Reading to Learn for ELs

Motivation Practices and Comprehension Strategies

for Informational Texts

Reading to Learn for ELs

Motivation Practices and Comprehension Strategies

for Informational Texts

ANA M. TABOADA BARBER

HEINEMANN
Portsmouth, NH

Heinemann

361 Hanover Street

Portsmouth, NH 03801–3912

www.heinemann.com

Offices and agents throughout the world

The author and publisher wish to thank those who have generously given permission to reprint borrowed material:

Excerpts from Common Core State Standards © Copyright 2010. National Governors Association Center for Best Practices and Council of Chief State School Officers. All rights reserved.

Figure 2–1: Gradual Release of Responsibility Model from "Essential Elements of Fostering and Teaching Reading Comprehension" by Nell K. Duke, P. David Pearson, Stephanie L. Strachan, and Alison K. Billman in *What Research Has to Say About Reading Instruction*, Fourth Edition, edited by S. Jay Samuels and Alan E. Farstrup. Copyright © 2011 by the International Reading Association, Inc. Reprinted with permission from the International Reading Association, Inc., conveyed through the Copyright Clearance Center, Inc.

How to Support ELs' Vocabulary Development: A Model of Instruction (with Figures 4–3 and 4–8) adapted from "The Effectiveness and Ease of Implementation of an Academic Vocabulary Intervention for Linguistically Diverse Students in Urban Middle Schools" by N.K. Lesaux, M.J. Kieffer, S.E. Faller, and J.G. Kelley originally appeared in *Reading Research Quarterly*, Volume 45, Issue 2 (2010). Reprinted with permission from Wiley.

Figure 6–8: Instructional Model of the FIST Strategy from "The Impact of Self-Questioning Strategy Use on the Text-Reader Assisted Comprehension of Students with Reading Disabilities" by G. Manset-Williamson, M. Dunn, R. Hinshaw, and J.M. Nelson originally appeared in the *International Journal of Special Education*, Volume 23, Issue 1 (2008). Adapted with permission from the *International Journal of Special Education.*

Figure 7–2: "QRAC-the-Code: A Comprehension Monitoring Strategy for Middle School Social Studies Textbooks" by Sheri Berkeley and Paul J. Riccomini originally appeared in the *Journal of Learning Disabilities*, Volume 46, Issue 2 (2013). Published by Sage Publications. Reprinted with permission from the publisher conveyed through the Copyright Clearance Center, Inc.

Photo credits:

Figure 2–4: Hispanic girl writting at desk in classroom. © Creatas/Getty Images; (platform) Platform of the Leicester Square underground station in London. © Eric Nathan/Alamy; (waiting area) Photodisc/Getty Images; (urban) Interior of Grand Central Station, New York City. © Keith Levit/Alamy; (rural) Morning commuters catching GO train in the Guildwood station in Toronto, Ontario, Canada. © Bill Brooks/Alamy; (airport) © Comstock Images/Getty Images; (bus station) Seattle Bus Station. © S. Meltzer/PhotoLink/Photodisc/Getty Images

Figure 2–5: Elementary student (6-7 years old) taking notes in laboratory. © Hero Images/Getty Images

page 61, photo by Natalie Brown

Cataloging-in-Publication Data is on file with the Library of Congress.

ISBN: 978-0-325-06251-8

Acquisitions Editor: Margaret LaRaia

Production Editor: Patty Adams

Cover design: Suzanne Heiser

Interior design: Shawn Girsberger

Typesetter: Shawn Girsberger

Manufacturing: Steve Bernier

Printed in the United States of America on acid-free paper

20 19 18 17 16 VP 1 2 3 4 5

To Lucas and Rusty,
whose love of books and learning engages my mind
in new ways, every day.

To my grandfather,
whose devoted teaching helped me become
a motivated learner.

Contents

PART 2 **INSTRUCTION IN ACTION: MODELS FOR MOTIVATION AND COMPREHENSION OF INFORMATIONAL TEXTS**

CHAPTER 3 **Background Knowledge and Self-Efficacy: Feeling Competent About What I Know and Can Do**

CHAPTER 4 **Vocabulary Learning and Knowledge Goals: Developing the Language of Experts**

CHAPTER 5 **Determining Importance: Main Ideas and Topic Relevance**

Message from Nell K. Duke

I know how to cook, at least the basics. I have a repertoire of strategies—marinating, mincing, and seasoning—for preparing food. I even know how to coordinate these strategies, such as mincing garlic for the marinade. But I don't *use* these strategies. In fact, I avoid cooking at all costs. When it comes to reading comprehension strategies in the classroom, many U.S. students are a lot like me in the kitchen. They know reading comprehension strategies. They can describe strategies, such as activating background knowledge, inferring, and self-questioning. They can even explain the importance of coordinating these strategies. But they don't actually *use* these strategies; in fact, they avoid reading at all costs.

Someone I know—who shall remain nameless—has a nearly opposite profile. He knows few traditional cooking techniques, let alone how to coordinate them, but is highly motivated to cook. The resulting concoctions, as you might imagine, are often not successful.

Ana Taboada Barber helps us take a major step forward in meeting the needs of both such profiles. She helps us recognize that motivational practices must go hand-in-hand with comprehension strategy instruction. It is not enough to teach students comprehension strategies; we must also use a variety of practices to motivate them to actually *use* the strategies. Yet it is not enough to motivate students; we must also teach them specific strategies that will help them channel their motivation into successful reading experiences.

Ana draws on the work of many researchers in education and psychology, as well as her own program of research, to articulate specific motivation practices to enact and comprehension strategies to teach. And she provides rich examples of the use of these practices in the classroom, with a particular focus on English Learners. If you are reading this letter, I don't need to tell you of the pressing need for all of us to learn more about how to better address the educational needs of English Learners. We are so fortunate to have Ana as our tutor in this work.

This book is a great fit for the *Research-Informed Classroom* series—bringing rigorous classroom-based research to bear on persistent challenges of classroom practice. The series aims to bridge the gap between research and practice by focusing on the most practical, classroom-relevant research and by communicating practices based on that research in a way that makes them accessible, appealing, and actionable. The series is founded on the belief that students and teachers are researchers' clients, and that serving them should be the highest priority.

Thank you, Ana, for providing this book, and thank you to everyone who reads it in their quest to help all ELs read to learn.

Nell K. Duke

Professor (and Frequent Take-Out Orderer)

Acknowledgments

Writing this book required the support of many people without whom it would not have been possible.

I thank Nell Duke for believing in my work and inviting me to be part of the Research-Informed Classroom series. Nell's facility for bridging research and practice is unique. Through Nell I met Margaret LaRaia, my wonderful editor at Heinemann. Margaret's talent for conveying ideas in practical, teacher-friendly words pushed my thinking about writing in new directions. I am grateful for the sincere and always kind way she shared her views. I learned much.

This work has been shaped by my interactions with mentors, teachers, late elementary and middle school students, parents, and graduate students over the last ten years. These encounters have influenced my understanding about reading motivation and comprehension. The inspiration I received from John T. Guthrie during my doctoral studies was invaluable. He is a truly motivated spirit who seeks to learn from every situation and approaches life with boundless enthusiasm. I've learned as much about motivating readers from listening to John as I've learned from watching him face life's joys and challenges.

The middle school teachers, students, literacy specialists, and administrators who eagerly tried new ideas as we developed our United States History for Engaged Reading (USHER) project were essential to my understanding of English Learners. The dedicated and creative graduate students who were part of the USHER project—Jori Beck, Leila Richey Nuland, Erin Ramirez, Melissa Gallagher, Peet Smith, Swati Mehta, Rebecca Caufman, and Lauren Serpati—were central to our success engaging English Learners (and English native speakers) with reading. I am particularly grateful to Peet Smith who gathered references, organized graphics and permissions, and steadfastly pursued other time-consuming tasks that helped make this book a reality.

The disciplined thinking and unwavering support of my colleague and dear friend Michelle Buehl helped me consider research questions and designs as we juggled the challenges of field work, data collection, and curricular implementation. The research conducted within the USHER project was funded by the Institute of Education Sciences (IES), United States Department of Education.

My research also would not have been possible without the generosity of late elementary teachers and their English Learners who tried out ideas and literacy practices that had worked with monolingual students. Their willingness to play along and their smiling "Buenos dias, Miss T!" greeting every morning made my experiences with implementation research deeply gratifying.

Writing a book is an incursion on family life, and my family has been unconditionally selfless. Finding clear ways and the right words to convey ideas took time away from my parents' visits from faraway Argentina. Their patience and their confidence in me have spanned my professional life. Without their unstinting support I would not be who I am today, nor would I enjoy the abundant benefits of bilingualism. In the midst of this project, my son, Lucas, was born, which meant navigating a new life with very different schedules while finding the time to write. Lucas' forgiveness and generosity were evident from the day he was born—I will always be grateful to him for allowing me to share his first year of life with my writing life. My husband, Rusty, has been unreservedly accommodating every step of the way. His support for my writing, ideas, and professional endeavors is immeasurable. I am grateful beyond words.

—Ana M. Taboada Barber
Silver Spring, MD

Introduction

Understanding the Comprehension Gap for ELs

It is true that English is a second language for me and that I experience less certainty communicating in English than I do in my native language, Spanish. However, the label of an English Learner (EL) would not be entirely accurate. I didn't begin learning English because I was an immigrant in an English-speaking country. Learning English was the result of my parents' choice. My mother spoke English fluently and believed in its value as a lingua franca—a *bridge language,* a language spoken worldwide that makes communication possible among people who do not share their first language. For me, learning English was an enrichment activity, a way to broaden my horizons

Although I still continue to develop my English-speaking skills, I also do so with my Spanish. I am bilingual. I speak, read, think, write, and even dream in two languages. Experience in two languages and cultures has given me a much wider range of possibilities and understandings. But for many students the benefits of bilingualism and biculturalism are invisible in schools, and they are instead uncomfortably aware of the large gap between their comprehension and that of their English-speaking peers. Because reading is at the basis of most learning, the inability to read and comprehend well affects our ability to learn new content, speak the "language of school," access certain jobs, communicate efficiently in the workplace, and, ultimately, compete in modern society. ELs' struggles with reading permeate all of their school lives. Without adequate explicit instruction and support from teachers, the distance between English Learner and bilingual/bicultural can feel like an impossible chasm to cross.

Labels can promote the lie of tidy understandings, especially when used to describe people. We're all so much more than what can be captured by one word or phrase. In education, diagnostic labels hold the danger of becoming fixed and limiting—struggling reader, English Learner, and so forth. A child is more than a struggling reader or an English Learner, and if we as educators do our jobs well, the label is time sensitive—true for only a brief period of time, as we support children in outgrowing the usefulness of that descriptor.

These labels *are* useful, of course, in identifying the support students require of us. Learning is an act with emotional and cognitive components. Learning a new language involves excitement for many, but also disorientation, struggle, and a lack of certainty: Did I communicate what I intended? Did I accurately understand what was communicated? What important information did I miss? When every school experience is marked by this uncertainty, not by success, ELs quickly become disengaged and their label dominates their potential for learning. What are ways to turn this around? How can we, as teachers, create classroom contexts that are guided by opportunities to read avidly and lead ELs to gain knowledge from text in engaging ways that lead to further learning? I wrote this book to help teachers find answers to these questions. I chose to specifically focus on the use of informational texts in ways that engage ELs because this work is essential in helping them succeed.

What Do We Know About the EL Student Population?

As I write this book, 4.4 million U.S. public school students are ELs (National Center for Education Statistics [NCES] 2014). And that number shows all signs of growing: by 2050, population projections predict 34% of children will be immigrants or children of immigrants, compared to 23% in 2005 (Passel and Cohn 2008). More and more teachers know what it means to have struggling EL students in their classrooms, but the knowledge on effective literacy instruction for ELs has not reached enough teachers, schools, and teacher education programs.

This gap for both EL students and their teachers is seen in our nationwide test data. On the 2013 National Assessment of Educational Progress (NAEP), 69% of fourth graders and 70% of eighth graders identified as ELs scored below the basic level in reading. In contrast, among non-EL students, 28% of fourth graders and 20% of eighth graders were below the basic level in reading (U.S. Department of

Education 2013). Inability to perform at the NAEP basic level implies challenges with locating relevant text information, making inferences, identifying main idea, theme, or author's purpose, and using understanding of text to identify details that support a given conclusion (National Assessment Governing Board 2010). But what do these statistics mean for the children who are ELs in your class right now, and what does it mean for you, their teacher? It means that we need to think about and design instruction that enables students to both meet and go beyond national standards.

Standardized tests, like the NAEP, and learning standards, like the Common Core State Standards (CCSS), help us identify specific learning goals and gaps for students across the country, including ELs. These standards require complex reading skills, such as close reading of a variety of complex texts and multiple inferential skills. Reading complex texts using these skills without appropriate help is too hard for ELs. Reading texts that are too hard and applying high-level cognitive skills without appropriate scaffolding can turn into a struggle that leads to destructive frustration, or a "collapse of motivation" (e.g., Snow 2013). However, although the CCSS call for high-level reading skills, they do not provide guidance on how to inspire students to pursue these complex tasks or purposes for learning. Without supports for engaged and motivated reading, achieving the standards will be especially challenging for ELs. Yet without the CCSS we have no way of holding ourselves accountable for equally challenging literacy standards for all students, English-native speakers and ELs alike. While the CCSS provide benchmarks for close, attentive reading of both literary and informational texts in language arts, social studies, and science, they leave room for teachers to decide how to achieve those goals (NGACBP and CCSSO 2010; Pearson 2013). This prerogative is invigorating but leaves many teachers at a loss, particularly regarding practices to support reading engagement. It is also beyond the scope of the CCSS to define the range of supports appropriate for ELs or for struggling readers (NGACBP and CCSSO 2010).

How This Book Can Help

I would guess you are reading this book because you are like many teachers I have met: You believe you might be able to do more for your ELs, and you may also believe the key to that work is to focus on comprehension of informational texts. Good, you're in the right place. Comprehension of informational texts becomes a steep challenge as ELs have to master language skills and content knowledge. However, success with informational texts is essential for students to meet content area standards. Language arts curricula include content-area literacy standards as early as kindergarten (Jeong, Gaffney, and Choi 2010), and about 50% of fourth-grade and 73% of eighth-grade texts on standardized tests are informational (Moss 2005). Also, informational texts are increasingly dominant in the digital world. With the omnipresence of the Internet, searches for all sorts of information take place continuously in every office and possibly many households all over the world. We know that ability to access, sift, summarize, and assess an increasing abundance of information, both in print and digitally, is needed to succeed in the workplace (Schmar-Dobler 2003) and to become conscientious, participating citizens in thriving democracies.

This kind of ease with informational texts is a high-leverage activity for ELs when it is supported within a thoughtful instructional framework. This book will provide you with that framework, but it will not do so in the form of a script or lesson templates. And it will not mean more work than you can handle. What you will see is that your work with students is more effective, that you and your students will see improvement in their comprehension of informational texts. In the first part of this book (Chapters 1 and 2) I explain the research on ELs' comprehension, the demands of content-area literacy, and how pairing motivation practices with comprehension strategies has been proven to improve ELs' comprehension. In the second part of the book (Chapters 3 through 8) I explain how to translate researched practices in comprehension and motivation with ELs into classroom practice. Each of these latter chapters pairs a reading comprehension strategy, such as activating background knowledge or asking text-based questions, with a motivation or engagement practice, such as providing meaningful academic choices or supporting students' self-efficacy. These pairings are offered to include a possible way to combine a comprehension strategy and a motivation practice, with a rationale for each based on research, and ways to weave them together and apply them to your teaching. However, these pairings are not prescriptive. Rather, as you become comfortable with motivation practices and comprehension strategies you are more likely to come up with pairings of these that work for you and your students. The important thing is not to obviate the fusion of motivation with cognitive tools! That is what fosters reading engagement.

This framework is based on the reading engagement model developed by John Guthrie and his colleagues (Guthrie et al. 1996) at the University of Maryland, and my own research in applying the engagement model to elementary and middle school ELs in the domains of science and social studies (Taboada et al. 2009; Taboada Barber et al. 2015). By the time you finish reading this book, my hope is that you will have the tools and knowledge to teach and show all students—especially your ELs in the late elementary to early middle grades—how to comprehend informational texts in effective ways and, more importantly, lead them onto becoming engaged readers of informational texts. Without this crucial skill, EL students can experience a learning gap that can increase over time.

The comprehension difficulties faced by ELs are closely intertwined with their challenges to become motivated to read and learn. Adolescents are particularly good at articulating this disengagement. Maria, a sixth-grade struggling reader EL, shared with me her struggles with reading when I asked her how she perceived herself as a reader: "I am not a very good reader. I know I could read more, and read better. But I do not like social studies. . . . I do not like all the information we have to learn. . . . My grandpa tells me I have to read history as a story, so I can remember more. . . . But how can I read it as a story when the sentences are so long and there are so many time lines that the teacher wants us to memorize? I get tired before starting to read!" Before she even begins reading a text, Maria already knows she's not interested. One reason might be that the tasks Maria is expected to do get in the way of her reading, specifically, memorizing a time line. Granted, the purpose of education is not only to deepen our existing strengths but to help us develop new skills, too. However, there are ways that we as teachers can be more thoughtful about designing reading tasks that engage our students and deepen their comprehension. If students do not experience success in reading, they are less likely to read. As all students, not just ELs, transition to middle school, the decline in academic motivation and performance increases (Anderman, Maehr, and Midgley 1999; Jacobs, Lanza, Osgood, Eccles, and Wigfield 2002; Wigfield, Eccles, Schiefele, Roeser, and Davis-Kean 2006). So, if we focus on nurturing the motivation to read, we can buffer students from trends of disengagement while deepening their comprehension of the texts they are reading in and out of school.

The Demands of Academic Literacy for ELs

When I was an English as a Second Language (ESL) teacher, I first noticed a trend starting in grade 3 among ELs of most backgrounds, but especially Spanish-speaking ELs (who make up between 73% and 80% of the total EL population in the US; NCES 2011). These students were capable word decoders but could not demonstrate deep comprehension of informational texts. In one-on-one conferences with these students I observed word automaticity, but I also observed monotone reading and student difficulty paraphrasing what they read. I carried this observation with me as I moved from teaching to research, and I ruminated upon it. For example, I asked Marcos, a fourth grader, to read the following paragraph to me from the book *Life Cycles of a Monarch Butterfly,* by Cooper, J. (2003).

> *Monarch migration is one of nature's most amazing stories. That's partly because monarchs are fragile and light. It would take about 800 monarchs to weigh a pound (.45 kilogram).* (Cooper 2003, p. 7)

Marcos struggled to describe what he had just read in his own words. He had no problem restating that butterflies were fragile and light. However, when asked why a monarch's weight might be important, Marcos could not link that detail to the concept of migration.

Marcos is not alone in this challenge. Identifying main ideas and connecting ideas within a short paragraph is a common difficulty among EL struggling readers. These challenges are in part related to vocabulary, but they are not limited to knowledge of word meanings. To make sense of a paragraph of several sentences, readers need to not only understand key word meanings but also get the meaning of each sentence, integrate information across successive sentences, and incorporate background knowledge to build coherent text representations (Cain and Oakhill 2009; Johnson-Laird 1983).

Most ELs tend to do quite well in the early grades on skills such as word decoding and phonological awareness. It is in later grades that difficulties with reading surface, particularly in the domains of vocabulary and comprehension (August, Shanahan, and Shanahan 2006). Starting in third grade, EL reading comprehension performance begins to decrease relative to national norms while their word reading skills tend to remain the same (Mancilla-Martinez and Lesaux 2010; Nakamoto et al. 2007; Proctor et al. 2005). By the time Spanish-speaking ELs reach grade 5, their text comprehension on average is at the second- or third-grade level. By age eleven, their vocabulary skills plateau at the level of an eight- to nine-year-old monolingual speaker (Mancilla-Martinez and Lesaux 2010). And this delay in comprehension skills tends to pervade most content areas. The problem becomes one of *academic literacy* (Torgesen et al. 2007), the kind of reading proficiency needed to construct meaning from content-area texts and that is assessed on state-level accountability measures. Comprehension skills within academic literacy include the ability to

- make inferences from text,
- summarize,
- identify relevant information,

- learn and apply new vocabulary from text, and
- read with a stance that pertains to a particular discipline (i.e., disciplinary literacy).

Although this is unquestionably a worrisome picture, it is in no way beyond teachers' ability to help students through appropriate instruction. Because struggles with reading for ELs often do not surface until the late elementary or middle grades, I focus on grades 3 through 8 in this book. That said, there is much teachers can do from preschool to grade 2 to lay the groundwork for text comprehension so that ELs do not have to play catch-up in grades 3 and beyond.

Why is reading comprehension strategy instruction for informational texts so necessary? In a way, comprehension of informational texts is the gateway to building the knowledge foundation for most disciplines. Without it children are severely limited in the knowledge they can acquire in science, social studies, and even math! Comprehension of informational texts improves students' understanding and retention of domain-specific information (Alvermann 2001; Biancarosa and Snow 2006; Kamil 2003; Heller and Greenleaf 2007; Torgesen et al. 2007). But there is evidence that shows that some teachers assume that learning English must precede content-area instruction (e.g., Collier 1989; Cummins 1981), an approach that inevitably causes ELs to fall behind their English-speaking peers (August and Hakuta 1997; García 1999). The variety of text structures used in informational texts (for example, compare and contrast, cause and effect, time lines), text features (for example, headings, captions, graphs/charts, diagrams), and content-specific vocabulary often make comprehension more difficult for students than narrative texts, whose structure and features are fewer and more familiar. Because the majority of the ESL teachers are unprepared to integrate English language and literacy with content-area instruction (Baker and Saul 1994; Stoddart et al. 2002), we need to provide clear models of integrated practice. For example, informational texts can be successfully used as read-alouds (Duke and Kays 1998), in guided and independent reading (Duke 2004), and in a variety of other authentic literacy practices, including communicating information to others and writing for specific purposes (Purcell-Gates, Duke, and Martineau 2007). Let's, again, take the case of Marcos, our fourth grader struggling with main idea identification. Marcos had achieved a relatively advanced level of English proficiency by fourth grade. He was able to communicate quite fluently, and his oral comprehension was almost at the level of an English native speaker. However, Marcos had not received consistent comprehension strategy instruction, and this showed in many of the challenges he encountered when reading informational texts, such as prioritizing information, determining a purpose for reading, and sharing information learned from texts in effective ways.

There is also growing research documenting the efficacy of integrating language arts with science (e.g., Cervetti et al. 2012; Guthrie et al. 2004; Pearson, Moje, and Greenleaf 2010) and literacy skills with social studies (e.g., De La Paz and Felton 2010; Halvorsen et al. 2012; Taboada et al. 2015). However, this integration is not well embedded in K–12 instruction (Pearson et al. 2013) where informational texts either have tended to be marginalized (Duke 2000) or are not part of common practice, especially with ELs (e.g., Taboada 2009). The purpose of this book is to provide a clear, actionable model for instruction.

ELs Need Compelling Reasons to Read Informational Texts

At any grade, teachers can play a critical role in supporting students' motivation for reading. Every teacher knows that students need to be motivated to learn. Opening a book, looking at its illustrations and connecting them to the text, striving to understand its content, and using or applying what one learns from it all require motivation—the effort, the persistence, the concentration, and the eagerness to learn. Going back to Marcos, I remember the pivotal moment when his teacher had him think about the relevance of learning about open and closed electric circuits. He understood that these circuits are key to how a light switch, a TV, a vacuum cleaner, and his computer worked, but he also understood that this knowledge was essential to avoiding an electrical hazard. Making this connection explicit to Marcos was crucial in motivating him to read further about electric circuits. Many teachers often believe that motivation comes from students' homes, which is sometimes true (Guthrie 2013). But for many students, including ELs who are struggling with language and literacy, the *intention to learn* may come from home but the supports for learning may be scarce. Teachers often underestimate the power they can play in fostering motivation in their own classrooms. Many research studies have shown that classroom contexts can be strong motivators (Guthrie, Wigfield, and Klauda 2012) and that with a bit of work and understanding of motivation principles and practices teachers can go a long way in encouraging motivated and engaged reading and learning.

Furthermore, researchers on motivation strongly believe that teachers ". . . can expand on how they enhance their students' motivation and learning. Even when they have not done so before, teachers can learn to give students a few meaningful choices—*choice within boundaries* is the idea. Teachers can promote partnership activities instead of constantly expecting solo work. Teachers can link a story or a science book to student backgrounds and personal interests to show relevance. Choice, collaboration, and relevance are all motivators—and there are dozens more (Guthrie and McPeake 2013). In this book, I share research-based principles on how to support ELs' engaged reading of informational texts.

Understanding the principles of motivation helps make our comprehension strategy instruction more targeted and successful. In Chapter 2 you'll learn essential principles of motivation, as well as an overview of some effective practices. For example, as an ESL teacher I was unaware that student choice—a widely used motivation practice—could motivate my students to become more involved in their reading and to read more deeply, so the choices my students were offered were arbitrary, and at times superficial. With time, I learned that choice works because it gives students a sense of control in their learning and that the choices offered had to be meaningful ones—not "Which color pen do you want to use for marking the text as you read?" but rather "How would you like to share with others what you learned from this book?" Meaningful choices involved upfront instruction so that students understood the purpose and reasons for choosing. Understanding the motivation principle helped define the parameters of my instruction.

ELs Need Explicit Strategy *and* Content Instruction

Comprehension strategies should not be separated from the teaching of content. Effective strategy instruction in the elementary and middle grades has shown that students benefit when key concepts within a topic are identified and comprehension strategy instruction becomes the vehicle for learning those key ideas within a topic or a domain (e.g., Taboada and Guthrie 2004). I write this book drawing from my experience in developing instructional materials that bridge literacy and science through my work on the development of Concept Oriented Reading Instruction (CORI), which was highly successful in increasing third, fourth, and fifth graders' reading comprehension and reading engagement in science (Guthrie, McRae, and Klauda 2007). One of the motivation-enhancing practices in CORI was *emphasizing knowledge content goals*. Third-, fourth-, and fifth-grade teachers taught students about ecological principles and key concepts in the domain of ecology as part of the core knowledge in life science. Students learned about predation, reproduction, competition, symbiosis, adaptation, and defense (Guthrie et al. 2004). Teaching about key concepts as content goals provides motivation for students because they have a purpose for using comprehension strategies with informational texts. By having content goals, students are compelled to use the strategies with greater effort, attention, and persistence as they are putting these at the service of learning content rather than using them in a context devoid of deep, conceptual themes (e.g., Wigfield et al. 2014).

Building on CORI, my colleagues and I developed United States History for Engaged Reading (USHER; Taboada Barber et al. 2015), an instructional framework that fused motivation supports such as autonomy support, relevance, small group collaboration, and self-efficacy with comprehension strategies such as questioning, activating background knowledge, and main idea identification to support reading comprehension in history for middle school English native speakers and ELs. In USHER we selected key history concepts from the state history curriculum and organized lessons to be driven by unit-specific concepts (e.g., *slavery, secession, economic growth/conflict, growth of monopolies*, etc.) so that comprehension strategies became tools for learning content related to these key concepts.

I draw from my experience with both instructional frameworks in this book, as they both have the common root in the reading engagement model (Guthrie and Wigfield 2000). Chapters 3 through 8 start with the assumption that we first plan what content we want to teach and then select the types of strategies that can help students learn that content (e.g., Gillis 2014; Herber 1970). You'll see how to provide ELs with explicit instruction of comprehension strategies and how to support their reading motivation to facilitate access to a variety of texts.

English Language Proficiency Informs Comprehension Strategy Instruction

As my work with students showed me, we do not need to wait for ELs to be fully proficient in English in order to teach them comprehension strategies to help with their understanding of informational texts (e.g., Taboada 2009; Taboada Barber et al. 2015). This idea agrees with empirical evidence indicating that when proficiency is developed in the first language, those skills can transfer to the second language (e.g., Cummins 1981; Lanauze and Snow 1989). In fact, there has been evidence that successful reader ELs transfer reading strategies across languages (Jimenez 1997). The importance of teaching comprehension strategies to ELs early on in their literacy development goes hand in hand with debunking the "learning to read/reading to learn" divide, given that students are always reading to learn.

In my experience, the teaching of ESL practices sometimes collides with the teaching of reading comprehension for ELs. This is not because ESL teachers do not see the importance of reading comprehension strategy instruction, but rather because they tend to put more of an emphasis on oral language proficiency instruction than on interaction with texts. This book is aimed for all teachers of ELs, including ESL teachers who have an interest in deepening their teaching of reading comprehension. Research on the oral language development and instruction of ELs offers several important principles that have an impact on successful comprehension strategy instruction. Among these, I highlight two that have direct bearing on the instructional ideas in this book.

First, it has been argued that excessive use of visuals such as graphic organizers, pictures, realia, and so forth can be misconstrued as "comprehensible instruction" (because of the nonverbal support provided) at the cost of getting around the language demands in academic texts (Harper and de Jong 2004). That is, although these accommodations can increase ELs' understanding of texts and simplify the complexity of academic language, teachers need to be aware that we should use them but recognize that they're insufficient. Why? Visual tools may sometimes fall short of meeting ELs' language needs. Depending on how they are used, nonverbal tools are limiting opportunities for language learning in content classes. Therefore, exposing ELs to multiple texts of varied reading levels is an important way of fostering their reading comprehension and language development. Furthermore, how to use those texts is even more important. We delve into appropriate uses of information texts later in the book.

Second, differing levels of biliteracy impact comprehension strategy instruction. ELs are individual students with their own patterns of language development who vary in their levels of biliteracy; this variation is often rooted in their academic experiences. For instance, ELs who are already literate and have a strong academic foundation in their L1 are likely to develop academic language skills earlier than social language skills in English. This challenges the belief that social language generally precedes academic language. Yet, although there is truth to this point, and ELs' biliteracy development is closely related to how much formal literacy instruction they have received in their first language, it is also true that EL's language proficiency in L1 and second language runs along a continuum (Gottlieb 2006). As such, there are predictable patterns within the continuum. The WIDA (Wisconsin-Delaware and Arkansas) Performance Definitions for Listening and Reading and for Speaking and Writing provide a good framework to think of language proficiency development as multidimensional (i.e., speaking, listening, reading, and writing) and running along a continuum (see Figures I–1 and I–2) within which certain milestones can be expected and should be fostered. Planning for ELs' literacy instruction should take into account their English proficiency as a continuum of skills as well as their literacy development in their first language. However, instruction should also take into account that students will tend to vary in their levels of proficiency in English and first language, with some dimensions such as oral language being more developed than others, such as reading, for example. Whenever possible, content area teachers should work closely with ESL teachers so they become aware of ELs' varying levels of proficiency along the biliteracy and language proficiency continua (see Figures I–1 and I–2). In other words, as with other dimensions of learning, we need to approach ELs' literacy development as a multifaceted endeavor for which students have formal and informal opportunities to learn and develop oral language. Writing and reading in each of their languages vary broadly based on the circumstances that have surrounded their academic and personal lives.

Figure I–1. WIDA Performance Definitions: Listening and Reading, Grades K–12

At each grade, toward the end of a given level of English language proficiency, and with instructional support, English language learners will process . . .

	Discourse Level	Sentence Level	Word/Phrase Level
	Linguistic Complexity	*Language Forms and Conventions*	*Vocabulary Usage*
Level 6: *Reaching language that meets all criteria through Level 5 Bridging*			
Level 5 Bridging	• Rich descriptive discourse with complex sentences • Cohesive and organized related ideas	• Compound, complex grammatical constructions (e.g., multiple phrases and clauses) • A broad range of sentence patterns characteristic of particular content areas	• Technical and abstract content-area language • Words and expressions with shades of meaning in each content area
Level 4 Expanding	• Connected discourse with a variety of sentences • Expanded related ideas	• A variety of complex grammatical constructions • Sentence patterns characteristic of particular content areas	• Specific, and some technical, content-area language • Words and expressions with multiple meanings of collocations and idioms for each content area
Level 3 Developing	• Discourse with a series of extended sentences • Related ideas	• Compound and some complex (e.g., noun phrase, verb phrase, prepositional phrase) grammatical constructions • Sentence patterns across content areas	• Specific content words and expressions • Words or expressions related to content area with common collocations and idioms across content areas
Level 2 Emerging	• Multiple related simple sentences • An idea with details	• Compound grammatical constructions • Repetitive phrasal and sentence patterns across content areas	• General, and some specific, content words and expressions (including cognates) • Social and instructional words and expressions across content areas
Level 1 Entering	• Single statements or questions • An idea within words, phrases, or chunks of language	• Simple grammatical constructions (e.g., commands, *Wh-*questions, declaratives) • Common social and instructional forms and patterns	• General content-related words • Everyday social and instructional words and expressions

. . . within sociocultural contexts for language use.

Note: Retrieved from https://www.wida.us/standards/

Figure I–2. WIDA Performance Definitions: Speaking and Writing, Grades K–12

At each grade, toward the end of a given level of English language proficiency, and with instructional support, English language learners will process . . .

	Discourse Level	Sentence Level	Word/Phrase Level
	Linguistic Complexity	*Language Forms and Conventions*	*Vocabulary Usage*
Level 6: *Reaching language that meets all criteria through Level 5 Bridging*			
Level 5 Bridging	• Multiple, complex sentences • Organized, cohesive, and coherent expression of ideas	• A variety of grammatical structures matched to purpose and nearly consistent use of conventions, including for effect • A broad range of sentence patterns characteristic of particular content areas	• Technical and abstract content-area language • Words and expressions with precise meaning related to content area topics
Level 4 Expanding	• Short, expanded, and some complex sentences • Organized expression of ideas with emerging cohesion	• A variety of grammatical structures and generally consistent use of conventions • Sentence patterns characteristic of particular content areas	• Specific and some technical content-area language • Words and expressions with multiple meanings or common collocations and idioms across content areas
Level 3 Developing	• Short and some expanded sentences with emerging complexity • Expanded expression of one idea or emerging expression of multiple related ideas	• Repetitive grammatical structures with occasional variation and emerging use of conventions • Sentence patterns across content areas	• Specific content words and expressions (including content-specific cognates) • Words or expressions related to content areas
Level 2 Emerging	• Phrases or short sentences • Emerging expression of ideas	• Formulaic grammatical structures and variable use of conventions • Repetitive phrasal and sentence patterns across content areas	• General content words and expressions (including common cognates) • Social and instructional words and expressions across content areas
Level 1 Entering	• Words, phrases, or chunks of language • Single words used to represent ideas	• Simple grammatical constructions (e.g., commands, *Wh-*questions, declaratives) • Phrasal patterns associated with common social and instructional situations	• General content-related words • Everyday social and instructional words and familiar expressions

. . . within sociocultural contexts for language use.

Note: Retrieved from https://www.wida.us/standards/

An Invitation

This book is for those teachers who are passionate about the teaching of reading and language—teachers who see reading as a door to endless opportunities for ELs' language and knowledge development; teachers who want and believe in engaging their students through and with reading; teachers who see reading as an infinite ocean of learning for their students. Comprehension strategy instruction and motivation practices are the ship that carries them on that journey.

As such, it is my hope that teachers reading this book see language proficiency development as multidimensional, as the WIDA standards conceive it, for which reading is an important dimension that feeds into the others—writing, listening, and speaking. Because they see it as a continuum, English proficiency levels are seen as fluid, providing indicators to guide their reading instruction (e.g., what text levels to choose).

In addition, this book is for teachers with varying backgrounds: reading teachers, content teachers, and ESL teachers. My experience has been with content-area literacy instruction, social studies, language arts, science, and even math! Teachers can be successful at teaching comprehension strategy instruction to their EL struggling readers. The common denominator among them is that they cared deeply about their students' reading and learning. Although I encourage content teachers to collaborate with ESL teachers to enhance ELs' overall language and literacy development, I am aware that curricula, time, and even building constraints not always make this possible. You can use the ideas and practices in this book whether you have a collaborative team or you are trying them on your own.

Lastly, this book tries to alleviate the anxiety that comes from trying to implement and deal with literacy and content standards simultaneously. We, and our students, can feel overwhelmed as we try to break down standards, objectives, and benchmarks into manageable daily steps. This book aims to help teachers who see the ambitious standards articulated by the CCSS and the large deficits reported on ELs as surmountable, because it will offer them specific, research-based steps to do so. We can create a joyful, successful place for all learners when we invite them to be curious, critical thinkers by showing them specific strategies and motivational practices that encourage them to become engaged readers.

PART 1

Research on What ELs Need for Success

Motivation Practices

Why the Desire to Know Matters

When we talk about student disengagement, we often view it in a narrow way by describing a student who isn't putting enough effort or focus into his schoolwork. We use vague language that keeps that student's actions distinct from our responsibility as teachers; it is behavior that is specific to the student, not to our instruction. But in that ambiguity lies our own dread: an awareness that our instruction might be failing our students. Most of us know that students are curious and want to discover new ideas. "It's wanting to know that makes us matter," Tom Stoppard wrote in his play *Arcadia.* When our students appear like they do not want to know, what they are really communicating is that we haven't invited them in; we haven't yet shown them that they matter. Take the case of Marina, a struggling fourth-grade reader who was part of my ESL class of fifteen students. Marina's father was a doctor and her mom was a biologist. At home, family discussions about health, live organisms, and environment preservation were abundant. Marina's curiosity about her natural environment was vast. She would often come to class with observations about a new plant in her home garden, the pollination of the daisies she had observed that morning, and how the birth of the puppies next door had been an eye-opening experience. However, as her teacher, I did not know how to cater to her interests. I would allow her to share these observations early in the day, but I did not follow up on them with texts that delved into those topics, or at least related to them. I felt committed to the ESL curriculum and the readings established in it. Marina was clearly indifferent toward reading isolated sentences to drill English grammar structures, the supermarket dialogue in the book that taught food item names, or the exchange between Johnny and his mom in the zoo that taught animal names. Although the ESL topics covered vocabulary needed for the ESL curriculum, none of these topics touched on Marina's interests. At that point I was insecure about walking away from the prescribed content and didn't think that having a few science books would be enticing to Marina in ways that the ESL curriculum was not—while still helping her with her English vocabulary! I couldn't figure out how to engage her with reading, how to cater to her thirst for learning.

The Challenges of Engagement and Motivation

The number of disengaged readers, especially in late elementary, middle, and high school, is not trivial. The 2011 Nation's Report Card reported that 46 percent of fourth graders said they read for fun almost every day, whereas only 8 percent of eighth graders did. Furthermore, the students in both grades who read for fun almost every day scored highest (proficient and advanced) on the NAEP reading tests; those who reported never or hardly ever reading for fun scored lowest (basic) (U.S. Department of Education 2011). This should not surprise us: engaged readers tend to be successful readers.

What skills do engaged readers tend to have and disengaged readers tend not to have? On the grade 4 NAEP, a "basic" score means that the student can make simple inferences and identify a main purpose/idea, whereas a "proficient" score describes a reader who can make complex inferences, compare ideas across texts, and draw conclusions. In grade 8, a "basic" score describes a student who can identify relevant text facts, whereas a "proficient" reader can interpret causal relations and recognize rhetorical devices. This listing of skills might seem abstract, but consider what happens when a student begins to accumulate a list of skills that he *cannot* do. The feeling of not achieving, not performing, or *cannot do* is highly demotivating. ELs often find themselves feeling that way: The challenges to make sense of text, often, seem insurmountable. For instance, note how the complexity of the standards for grades 4 and 5 increases—for both CCSS and NAEP (Figure 1–1)—from identification of main idea and supporting details to integrating information across texts to finally drawing simple and complex inferences from text. Both sets of standards, CCSS and NAEP, communicate the expectation that each grade level will require achievement of new and complex skills. It is easy to infer how academic difficulty becomes academic disengagement as the gap between what the EL knows and can do and what is expected of him widens without support.

Figure 1–1. CCSS and NAEP Informational Text Standards

NAEP Grade 4	CCSS Grades 4–5
Fourth-grade students performing at the **basic** level should be able to: - Identify the main purpose and an explicitly stated main idea. » Gather information from various parts of a text to provide supporting information. Fourth-grade students performing at the **proficient** level should be able to: - Locate relevant information. - Integrate information across texts. - Compare ideas across two texts. - Evaluate the way an author presents information. - Demonstrate an understanding of the purpose for text features. - Integrate information from headings, text boxes, and graphics and their captions. Fourth-grade students performing at the **advanced** level should be able to: - Make complex inferences about main ideas and supporting ideas. - Express a judgment about the text and about text features and support the judgment with evidence. - Identify the most likely cause given an effect. - Explain an author's point of view.	By the end of year, read and comprehend informational texts, including history/social studies, science, and technical texts, in the grades 4–5 text complexity band proficiently, with scaffolding as needed at the high end of the range: - Determine the main idea of a text and explain how it is supported by key details; summarize the text. - Describe the overall structure (e.g., chronology, comparison, cause/effect, problem/solution) of events, ideas, concepts, or information in a text or part of a text. - Integrate information from two texts on the same topic in order to write or speak about the subject knowledgeably. - Use text features and search tools (e.g., key words, sidebars, hyperlinks) to locate information relevant to a given topic efficiently. - Interpret information presented visually, orally, or quantitatively (e.g., in charts, graphs, diagrams, time lines, animations, or interactive elements on web pages) and explain how the information contributes to an understanding of the text in which it appears. - Refer to details and examples in a text when explaining what the text says explicitly and when drawing inferences from the text. - Use text features and search tools (e.g., key words, sidebars, hyperlinks) to locate information relevant to a given topic efficiently. - Explain events, procedures, ideas, or concepts in a historical, scientific, or technical text, including what happened and why, based on specific information in the text. - Explain how an author uses reasons and evidence to support particular points in a text.

Figure 1–1. CCSS and NAEP Informational Text Standards *(continued)*

NAEP Grade 8	CCSS Grades 6–8
Eighth-grade students performing at the **basic** level should be able to: • Recognize inferences based on main ideas and supporting details. • Locate and provide relevant facts to construct general statements about information from the text. • Provide some support for judgments about the way information is presented. Eighth-grade students performing at the **proficient** level should be able to: • Locate and provide facts and relevant information that support a main idea or purpose. • Interpret causal relations. • Provide and support a judgment about the author's argument or stance. • Make connections within and across texts to explain causal relations. • Evaluate and justify the strength of supporting evidence and the quality of an author's presentation. • State and justify judgments about text features and choice of content to convey meaning. • Justify the author's use of evidence and rhetorical devices.	By the end of year, read and comprehend informational texts, including history/social studies, science, and technical texts, at the high end of the Grades 6–8 text complexity band independently and proficiently: • Cite textual evidence to support analysis of what the text says explicitly as well as inferences drawn from the text. • Analyze in detail how a key individual, event, or idea is introduced, illustrated, and elaborated in a text (e.g., through examples or anecdotes). • Determine a central idea of a text and how it is conveyed through particular details; provide a summary of the text distinct from personal opinions or judgments. • Determine a central idea of a text and analyze its development over the course of the text, including its relationship to supporting ideas; provide an objective summary of the text. • Determine an author's point of view or purpose in a text and explain how it is conveyed in the text. • Compare and contrast a text to an audio, video, or multimedia version of the text, analyzing each medium's portrayal of the subject (e.g., how the delivery of a speech affects the impact of the words). • Determine an author's point of view or purpose in a text and analyze how the author acknowledges and responds to conflicting evidence or viewpoints. • Analyze in detail the structure of a specific paragraph in a text, including the role of particular sentences in developing and refining a key concept. • Determine the meaning of words and phrases as they are used in a text, including figurative, connotative, and technical meanings; analyze the impact of specific word choices on meaning and tone, including analogies or allusions to other texts.

Source: From the National Assessment of Educational Progress (NAEP) 2011 Reading Framework. Test specifications and methodology developed by the National Assessment Governing Board, appointed by the U.S. Secretary of Education.

As we discussed in the Introduction, making progress on these skills requires persistence in reading complex texts, reading closely, and using reading strategies that increase comprehension. These new benchmarks hold ELs to higher standards, which is good, but without the appropriate scaffolding ELs are only aware of expectations they cannot meet. It is always important to remember that the standards are not only for measuring what students know and can do, but also for measuring what and how we teach them. Here's an example of how those high standards without support may also affect the way students perceive themselves as readers. When asked whether he saw himself as a good reader, fourthgrader Juan said:

> Nahh. I only read when I am asked to do it in school. I understand reading is important for school and work, but reading the science textbooks can be really hard. And social studies, I just don't like. [The book] is long and there are new words to me, and I get confused if I am asked too many things to do.

The more challenging the materials and skills to master, the more struggling readers will tend to disengage because they don't know how to re-engage or persist through text difficulty—and often because they don't have sufficient reason to do so. We know that students will persist through difficult texts if they are more motivated to do so. For example, researchers have shown us that children's reading motivation relates to their performance in reading (Baker and Wigfield 1999; Wigfield and Guthrie 1997) and that when students are motivated to read they achieve more (Campbell, Voelkl, and Donahue 1997). Furthermore, children who are motivated to read for intrinsic reasons (e.g., wanting to learn more about a topic) will tend to persist through challenging texts using higher-order reading strategies (Guthrie, Van Meter, McCann, et al. 1996). However, as students move toward the upper grades, their motivation for school in general, and for reading in particular, tends to drop (Gottfried 1985; Gottfried et al. 2007). In a districtwide survey of seventh graders, 80 percent indicated that informational texts in science, social studies, and math were "boring." What does it mean when students, particularly low-performing students, say they are bored? The seventh graders surveyed elaborated on their boredom by explaining that they exerted little effort and avoided reading whenever possible (Guthrie, Wigfield, and Klauda 2012). Boredom also comes from the nature of the tasks and the texts students are asked to perform in relation to informational texts. For instance, many of the informational texts used in the later elementary grades and beyond are just not interesting to students. Nearly 80 percent of high-achieving and 70 percent of lower-achieving students report that they are not interested in the information books that they read in school (Guthrie, Klauda, and Morrison 2012). Tasks such as responding to teacher questions to show text understanding or complete a book report are also uninteresting to many students. The combination of disinterest in what they read and the perception that school texts are difficult is not conducive to engaged or motivated reading (Wigfield et al. 2014). The only way to overcome the detachment of boredom is the attachment of motivation. We can't just expect our students to "toughen up and grit their way through it" because that implies motivation. In other words, the essential scaffold for all learning is motivation. Our struggling EL readers require school and teacher support to increase their motivation to read, as much if not more than anyone.

In fact, the CCSS require challenging and rigorous tasks intended to evaluate the products of close reading, but many curricular units designed to meet the standards are clearly lacking attention to student interest or precursor activities (e.g., discussion of popular culture or personal experience events) that can, at least, elicit interest and motivate close reading (e.g., Snow 2013). Some researchers have argued that literacy engagement is the missing link in implementing the standards: "Because complex texts are so challenging students have to [. . .] want to unlock deeper meanings of complex literary and informational texts in order to succeed at career readiness as it is proposed by the CCSS" (Guthrie and McPeake 2013, 162). If the challenging tasks required by the CCSS are not guided or started by practices such as engaging questions, appealing topics, and important issues (e.g., Guthrie, Klauda, and Ho 2013; Snow 2013), many students are likely to lose interest and engage in shallow, superficial reading. In fact, when instruction includes such engagement practices in combination with consistent multiple strategy instruction (e.g., inferencing, summarizing, and graphic organizing of key concepts) such as in CORI, middle school students have been found to increase their information text comprehension through increasing self-efficacy and decreasing perceived difficulty. That is, instruction that is designed to fuse motivation and cognitive practices increases students' confidence in their capacity to succeed and decreases students' perceptions of texts being too challenging to comprehend (Guthrie, Klauda, and Ho 2013). All in all, a motivated *reader* is a motivated *learner*. Reading comprehension is essential for success, not just in reading class but also in all other subjects in school (Wigfield et al. 2014). Children who struggle with reading are very likely to struggle with many other dimensions of learning. That struggle leads to indifference and disengagement. In fact, the academic struggles of ELs are mostly due to struggles with reading comprehension (e.g., Lesaux et al. 2010; Mancilla-Martinez and Lesaux 2011). When

Juan struggles to understand the causes of the civil war, he is struggling with vocabulary, abstract concepts, syntactic structures, and dense text. Faced with so many areas of challenge, Juan feels like giving up easily; persevering with text is not something he would initiate or truly consider. The roads to not understanding are too many. He needs help to become hooked into reading.

When Juan's teacher works to help Juan become *motivated to read* about the Civil War, she is ultimately creating the classroom context for Juan to be immersed in the act of learning, of building key concepts about the causes, development, and consequences of the Civil War—for which reading is a crucial tool. Juan, in turn, becomes motivated to read informational text when he feels compelled to discuss his learning from the text with others and connects his reading to previous learning. Engaged reading is purposeful learning, driven by the reader's desire to know.

How Can We Support ELs' Motivation to Read?

I use the word *immersed* to describe engagement because it communicates stepping into something beyond oneself. A reader who becomes immersed in the act of reading is confident enough to step into a text. He knows that he may be confused by concepts or language and that he may be challenged by new ideas. Yet he is confident enough in himself, and in the belief of what he may gain, that he is willing to dip into the uncertainty of a new text. That willingness, that desire, comes from within; it is intrinsic, or self-initiated, motivation. When a child reads for extrinsic reasons—such as pizza points, avoiding punishment, or earning a grade—she disengages when the task is done and the reward is offered or the threat of punishment removed. When a child's motivation to read is appropriately fostered in classroom contexts, her reading is likely to spring within the classroom and continue beyond the boundaries of school-assigned tasks. However, without the motivation to hone advanced cognitive skills and learn from complex texts, reading becomes a cold, cognitive exercise for struggling ELs and their challenges go unsupported. That is, if students are not motivated to read and not supported by their teachers to do so, they are deprived of the willingness to dig into text and learn more. They read less for their own sake or to pursue their own interests, and their reading becomes subject to teacher or test requirements. They are constrained by performing the task at hand and are less inclined to transfer skills and knowledge to new situations and contexts.

The good news is that abundant research with English native speakers (e.g., Guthrie et al. 2004, Guthrie, McRae, and Klauda 2007) and more recently with

ELs (Taboada and Rutherford 2011; Taboada Barber et al. 2015) shows that teachers can support motivation and engagement in many ways in the classroom and beyond, helping students to not only develop the cognitive skills they need to meet the CCSS but, more importantly, sustain and deepen these skills over time and be inclined to use them. For example, motivation can be supported through the use of meaningful text choices, explanations for the value of learning-specific content and comprehension strategies, or setting knowledge goals by providing opportunities to learn about the same topics in depth and over time. In sum, supports for motivated and engaged reading work in tandem with the enhancement of cognitive skills for reading. Motivated and engaged reading helps students (a) learn cognitive skills, such as when self-efficacy or feeling competent helps with effortful, challenging reading via use of higher-order strategies; (b) deepen the development of cognitive skills over time, such as when student interests and open-ended questions are conducive to challenging tasks like close reading; and (3) be inclined to employ cognitive skills that may otherwise become inert or not used (Hall and Sabey 2007), such as when students who are intrinsically motivated to read are inclined to use comprehension strategies (e.g., Guthrie et al. 1996).

Some Important Distinctions

Motivation and engagement are often superficially described as "fun." This confusion arises because there are many learning activities that are cute, involving making things or movement, but without a strong connection to the longer-term purposes of learning. The words *motivation* and *engagement* are often used interchangeably, but they are not synonymous. *Motivation* is the desire or predisposition that energizes and directs student behavior and usually refers to their beliefs, values, and goals related to various activities (Eccles and Wigfield 2002; Wigfield et al. 2006). When a student believes that effort is directly related to his learning instead of, say, just his aptitude or intelligence, he displays a motivational belief about his learning. He believes that learning is related to the effort and persistence one puts into it. *Engagement* is more encompassing than motivation; it is an umbrella term that includes dimensions of students' behavior, cognition, and their affect or emotions (Fredricks, Blumenfeld, and Paris 2004). While motivation refers to the willingness, the desire, to invest time and effort in learning, engagement refers to the student's actual participation or involvement in learning or reading (Gettinger and Walter 2012).

Reading engagement is the degree to which students process text deeply using cognitive strategies and prior knowledge in strategic and motivated ways (Guthrie and Wigfield 2000). Engaged readers are motivated to read, approach text strategically, know how to construct meaning from what they read, and talk about what they've read with their friends and family (Guthrie et al. 1996; Guthrie and Wigfield 2000). In this book I'll revisit aspects of motivation and engagement as they pertain to reading, specifically to reading of informational text (see Figure 1–2). What follows is a fuller explanation of five motivation practices that we can use to enhance the literacy instruction of ELs. These motivation practices include self-efficacy, relevance, knowledge goals, autonomy, and student collaboration. We'll revisit these motivation practices within specific instructional ideas in Chapters 3 through 8.

Self-Efficacy: Developing ELs' Competence for Specific Tasks

To support students' self-efficacy, we must know our students well so that we can assess their skills to tailor our instruction to their needs. Albert Bandura (1997), the originator of the concept, defines self-efficacy as an individual's belief in his or her capability to execute the actions needed to succeed in specific tasks or situations. Students' belief in their ability to succeed in specific academic situations or tasks is related to their choices, their persistence, how they feel about a specific task or activity, and ultimately how well they perform it. When we hear a sixth-grade student like Tomás state, "I want to read more about monarch butterflies' migration because I am still not clear on how such little things can survive such a long trip! Can I read a book with more information on this?" we know Tomás is choosing a topic that takes his learning further and is aligned with an interest he has clearly identified after some initial reading. Tomás' choice to deepen his knowledge denotes engagement with the topic of monarch butterflies

Figure 1–2.   Motivation Practices that Foster Engaged Reading in ELs

Self-efficacy	How can I develop competence through specific tasks?
Relevance	How does his learning matter for the ELs in my classroom?
Knowledge goals	How can I promote a mindset for growth through mastery goals?
Autonomy	How can I provide meaningful academic choices to scaffold independent reading?
Collaboration	How can I structure collaboration so that ELs feel supported to reach beyond themselves for meaning?

but, more specifically, it demonstrates a strong sense of efficacy and competence about what he can and cannot do. He is confident about his reading in science. He has enough background knowledge—and curiosity—about the monarchs that leads to his choice. He is pretty sure he can understand the topic well, or is willing to try to do so. Tomas' choosing and wanting to read further springs from his beliefs about what he can do as a reader. He is confident he can take his learning a bit further. His choices of topics or texts are influenced by his self-efficacy, his beliefs of what he can accomplish as a reader. Just like self-efficacy affects the choices our students make, it also has an impact on whether they persist on a task or not, and how well they do it. Think of an activity or a task that you really feel good at doing. Are you likely to persist on it or give it up easily in the face of adversity? Now think of an activity you really do not feel confident in doing—how likely are you to persist on it? How would your performance compare on the one you feel competent at versus the latter? Self-efficacy is a big factor in determining our persistence, determination, and ultimate performance on a task.

To help students develop their self-efficacy for various academic tasks we must provide many opportunities for students to broaden their sense of competence, to develop their skills, and to build their knowledge of skills and their capabilities over time.

Students who have a great deal of confidence in their capability to do a specific activity usually perform it well. If their confidence is low, their effort, perseverance, and engagement are usually low. Reading self-efficacy is related to students' choice of reading material (length, difficulty), how diligently they try to understand the text, their comprehension of the material, and ultimately what they learn from reading. Struggling readers often do not fully grasp what it takes to succeed. ELs may believe they just aren't good at it; they may see it as something that better readers do. When we help students set goals that are challenging but realistic, we show them incremental ways they can improve—we create a map.

Because self-efficacy beliefs are context specific, we have to pay close attention to our students. A student may feel confident about browsing a text and identifying text features, but he may not be confident in his ability to identify the main idea in a paragraph or summarizing a page. Then, too, students' self-efficacy beliefs may not reflect their actual skill. Some students, especially ELs, do not recognize that they possess the skills to be successful. Others believe they can do a task when they cannot. We need to lead students to recognize the skills and abilities they have, as well as those needing further development.

Tomás, the sixth grader you met earlier, feels confident about his reading of science texts. He has plenty of background knowledge about certain topics, such as insect survival, which serves to deepen his interests and take his learning on this topic further. However, he feels weaker about social studies; in particular, he has difficulty remembering details when discussing time lines and sequenced events. Ms. Martin, his social studies and language arts teacher, is aware of this, so she works closely with Tomás to strengthen this skill by helping him see his step-by-step improvements on sequencing information.

Although most of the research on reading engagement has been conducted with English-speaking populations (e.g., Guthrie et al. 2004; Morgan and Fuchs 2007), the sixth and seventh graders my colleagues and I worked with in our USHER project included a large number of ELs, mostly Spanish-speaking. When we break strategies into steps and follow the gradual release of responsibility (GRR) model—clear modeling, guided practice, frequent independent use— even students who think of themselves as poor readers can be explicitly taught to refine the skills required for specific tasks. They can also be encouraged to develop their abilities to succeed. We've found that cognitive strategy instruction coupled with supports for self-efficacy increases the literacy engagement and reading comprehension of all students, especially ELs who read below grade level (Taboada Barber et al. 2015). Supports for self-efficacy for sixth and seventh graders involved step-by-step comprehension strategy instruction with specific feedback for individual students along the way. It also fostered a deeper understanding of what tasks comprise the ability to read effectively—for example, reading fluently versus reading in a choppy manner.

Because self-efficacy consists of our beliefs about how well we can do a task, understanding the steps or components of the task is essential to self-efficacy. In addition, in USHER we provided contingent feedback on their reading so that students could monitor their progress over time while also understanding which components of their reading needed more work than others (e.g., fluency development versus summarization). Furthermore, we found that sixth- and seventh-grade English monolinguals and ELs who struggled with reading increased in their reading self-efficacy as a result of teachers' support for this practice during the three months that the USHER program was in place. The increase in students' confidence in their reading capabilities was more striking than it was for students who did not receive teachers' supports for efficacy beliefs in a comparison group. Not surprisingly, English native speakers as a group had higher reading efficacy beliefs than ELs, yet all students' self-efficacy, irrespective of their language status, improved as a result of teacher supports for reading efficacy, such as use of specific praise and feedback on components of various reading tasks (Taboada Barber et al. 2015). The majority of these teachers were able to grasp the idea that self-efficacy is not so much about learning *how* to succeed as it is about learning *how to persevere when one does not succeed* at a given task. "Self-efficacy cannot provide the skills required to succeed (these still need to be taught!), but it can provide the effort and persistence required to obtain those skills and use them effectively" (Pajares and Urdan 2006, 345). In Chapter 3 I provide the case of Melissa, a fifth-grade EL who struggles with self-efficacy for reading, so you can have a sense of how low self-efficacy affects learning and reading. I also describe Vanessa Shann's instruction supporting Melissa's and other ELs' self-efficacy for reading in relation to a specific comprehension strategy: activating background knowledge. Figure 1–3 provides some guidelines on promoting self-efficacy for learning in general and for reading in particular.

Figure 1–3.   Instruction That Promotes Self-Efficacy in Reading

Make students aware that new learning can be confusing and that making mistakes is part of the learning process. Share self-efficacy stories. Let students know how you have struggled to learn or do something, but how your belief in yourself helped you overcome a failure or obstacle.

Teach comprehension strategies. Teach specific comprehension strategies in explicit and cumulative ways. Name the strategy and explicitly state how it helps comprehension. ("Activating background knowledge helps me read more closely as I make connections between what I know and what I read.") Model the strategy so students see the process. Making the strategy more visible helps the student understand what she or he can do while reading.

Model "coping." Struggle while reading a passage, thinking through the challenges out loud and showing how you use a particular strategy to solve them. This encourages students to rethink their own work.

Provide supportive, specific language to help students find a way through struggle. Don't say, "Saying it that way makes you sound dumb" or "Do it like I showed you." Say, "You may want to say it this way; it's easier for others to understand" or "What ways do you think may work?"

Let students solve problems or complete challenging activities in their own way, as much as possible. Allot time based on the difficulty of the task and the degree of student involvement.

Use informational rather than controlling language. Provide reasons for specific requests or actions. Instead of commanding, "One, two, three, eyes on me," provide a reason: "You need to pay attention now because this is important for your learning." Don't always direct focus to you as the teacher. Instead of saying, "Because I say so," offer reasons for your requests: "It's the most time-efficient way." "It's the best way for you to learn this concept."

Provide task-specific, informational feedback. Explain why a response is correct or incorrect; for example, "That is incorrect, because you did not include . . . ."

Be judicious about praise. Offer praise only when it is deserved; undeserved praise is not effective. Praising a student who links her background knowledge to an idea in text supports her self-efficacy for activating background knowledge.

(continues)

Figure 1–3.   Instruction That Promotes Self-Efficacy in Reading *(continued)*

Compare students with their own progress over time (e.g., last week/month versus this one) rather than with one another. Encourage students to attribute their performance to internal, controllable factors (e.g., effort, strategy use) rather than uncontrollable factors (e.g., ability). Be sure that students link their effort to the outcome.

Help students recognize when their comprehension skills need improvement. For example, if a student misidentifies the main idea of a passage, shape his thinking by pointing out what the process is, where he went wrong, and how to correct the mistake. Asking him to explain his reasoning may help you identify the problem. Provide feedback that is specific enough that students can improve their skills and understand what they are doing right or wrong. Rather than say, "Mark, I really like your reading," say, "Mark, I really like the types of questions you are asking. They make me think about complex explanations."

Provide explicit instruction and opportunities to practice. If taught well and used consistently, the gradual release of responsibility model can be a great model to foster self-efficacy for reading.

Have clear procedures on "what to do" for different activities. Make the *what* and *how* of your literacy instruction clear. Clarity about procedures helps break up tasks into steps and build self-efficacy for different components of a task.

Relevance: Connecting Learning to ELs' Lives and Discussing "Why"

We connect students to new learning from two directions: by knowing who our students are and by getting our students to believe in the value of the content they are learning. That thread of connection is established by communicating relevance. Students need to see learning as important to their interests, goals, and values: "Teachers may explain the contribution of the learning task to students' personal goals and attempt to understand students' feelings and thoughts concerning the learning task" (Assor, Kaplan, and Roth 2002, 264). Relevance is key in teaching all subjects, but some require it more than others.

As part of our research, my colleagues and I explored sixth and seventh graders' view of history. Many disliked it: "It's something from the past. I don't know how it helps me today." Rita reflects on the lecture model as one that leaves her "bored" and disengaged: "The way my teacher teaches history is through a lot of talking, so I get bored; it's not something that interests me." Similarly, Miguel finds the absence of interesting texts and extensive teacher talk or lecturing as tiring: "I don't know what we're really learning. I can't concentrate when the teacher talks for so long, and the book is so boring." We can anticipate and prevent these kinds of statements by making relevance a theme of our instruction (see Figure 1–4). Helping students see the relevance of academic activities doesn't consist only of providing interesting activities; students need to understand the

Figure 1–4. Instruction That Communicates Relevance

Present tasks and content enthusiastically. If you don't treat the task or content as important and meaningful, neither will your students.

Ask students to think about how specific events, topics, and artifacts relate to their own experiences or lives.

Ask students to explain the reason for using specific reading strategies. ("Why do we need to ask questions before or during reading? Why do we care about finding the main idea in a paragraph or page?")

Ask how and why questions to help students voice their own thinking and establish connections over time.

Explain or discuss the value of learning about a topic and its relation to students' lives today. How does history relate to current events and topics? ("How do the Articles of the Confederation relate to life today? Why do we need to know about the European explorers that came to North America?") How is a science experiment relevant to health or the environment?

Encourage discussion focused on understanding, elaborating on and applying what students have learned.

Ask students to think through the relevance of a topic and, as a group, determine three reasons the topic is important.

reasons for these tasks or topics. Explanations of why it's important to use specific reading strategies or learn about American Indian tribes or the Articles of the Confederation give these activities meaning, and give students a sense of control over their learning. When we do this we infuse our instruction with a reason to know.

The relevance of history topics being learned powerfully connects students to their identities as citizens (Beck, Taboada Barber, and Buehl 2013). When Miguel was asked whether and why it's important to learn about American history, he said: "Because if you go to like a different country or something and they ask you some questions you don't want to say, 'Oh, I don't know anything about my country' and stuff like that." Miguel's answer implies the broader purpose of understanding the history of his country so he can have an intelligent discussion with people from other countries. Sixth-grader Diana was excited to learn about American Indians because of her heritage: "And then also I'm one-sixteenth Native American. So I'm really interested in learning about that 'cause then I can learn about my own tribe and stuff." She had a direct connection to early American history and wanted to learn about it. Sixth-grader Luis found history important as a way to learn from past mistakes: "If we don't learn history, we will make the same mistakes in the future that we made in the past. History helps us not to repeat them. If we see why we went [to war] before, maybe we cannot go again." Marisa discovered that learning history develops a sense of citizenship: "If I know my country's history well, I can better help my country when I have to vote for president or understand why people fight for laws in the government." We can switch students' perceptions of social studies from dry history to a powerful catalyst that helps students reflect on their identities.

Establishing relevance for learning can go beyond content and expand to reasons for using specific reading tools, such as reading strategies. These are especially helpful to struggling readers. Having a reason for using a reading strategy makes the activity meaningful—it lets students see why they are doing it. Why is the "why" of the activity important? The messages we communicate, whether intentional or unintentional, affect students' engagement and their learning goals and outcomes (Graham and Golan 1991) as well as shape their interests and intrinsic motivation (Reeve and Jang 2006). For example, think of autonomy-supportive versus controlling behaviors and the language that accompanies them. It is very different if we use controlling language that, for instance, utters solutions or answers such as "We activate background knowledge this way, like this . . ." than if we use language that provides students with information or rationales such as "How about we try activating what we know about this topic because it is going to help us with better understanding of . . . ." Students feel much more compelled to listen to you if you provide a reason for why they should, even if this is simple and related to their academics. In Chapter 5 I describe some ways in which teachers can foster relevance both for content and for comprehension strategies. I do it in the context of social studies, a subject area that many students, and many ELs in particular, see as disconnected from their lives and interests. In the same chapter I also provide some guidelines on how to weave together, the comprehension strategy of identifying main ideas and relevance as a motivation practice.

Knowledge Goals: Promoting ELs' Mindset for Growth

Students' learning goals affect their effort, engagement, self-efficacy, interest, and anxiety, even how they respond to mistakes (Alderman 2008). Students who focus on mastering a task and growing in knowledge, not on how well they perform the task compared with others, are more motivated and engaged, better adjusted to school life (Pintrich 2000).

Here's how three seventh graders approach reading aloud in front of their classmates:

Maria: *I've always felt insecure about reading in front of other students, so practicing oral reading in this class will help me prepare to present a reading at our end-of-year celebration. It will also help me to learn more.*

Andrea: *After I read aloud two or three times, everyone will see that I am the best reader in this class.*

Pedro: *I just hope I don't make a fool of myself and my oral reading is not the worst in the class and the teacher gives me a passing grade.*

Maria wants to master her ability to read; she also sees reading as a tool for learning, for building knowledge. Andrea wants to appear competent and smart. Pedro doesn't want to look incompetent or dumb. Maria will achieve the most positive outcome because she sees an intrinsic value in the activity.

Motivational researchers use terms such as *learning, task, task-involved, mastery and knowledge goals* to refer to goals that orient the student to focus on the task in terms of mastering or learning how to do the task (Pintrich 2000), to develop and grow in knowledge about a task or content. These terms stand in contrast to labels such as *performance, relative ability*, and *ego-involved goals*, which have been used to refer to goals that orient the individual to focus on the self, ability, or performance relative to others (Pintrich 2000). In this book, I use the term *knowledge goals* to refer to students focusing on the task at hand and on the knowledge they can acquire from reading, rather than their abilities or performance. The terms *mastery* and *knowledge goals* are highly related, but they are not the same. Knowledge goals are readily related to reading informational texts, whereby the goal is to have readers delve into reading and build knowledge, or learn from text. Mastery goals are more comprehensive, describing a student orientation as more focused on learning for the sake of learning than on grades or outcomes, and on enjoying the challenge of the tasks engaged in. Most students have a combined orientation toward mastery and performance. Maria is motivated to improve her oral reading (mastery), and to learn more through reading (knowledge building) while also wanting to perform well at the end-of-year celebration (performance). But if a student's concern for performance is consistently stronger than her concern for mastery, it's a good bet it will lessen her motivation and engagement (Alderman 2008; Pintrich 2000). If Maria was mostly driven to outperform her classmates on reading and there was no inner drive for learning, her engagement with learning from reading would likely wither over time.

Two main factors affect goal orientation: how the student views intelligence (Dweck and Leggett 1988; Molden and Dweck 2000) and contextual influences such as classroom structure. One theory about intelligence is that it is an entity, something we have. Children with this view need to demonstrate that they are smart, and protect their ability. If they fail at an academic task, they can attribute the failure to not being smart enough rather than to having tried and failed. They give up. Many struggling readers see the ability to read in this light—"I am not a good reader"—and resign themselves to it. A second theory about intelligence is that it is malleable or susceptible to change. Children with this view see effort as crucial to their academic endeavors and are more likely to focus on developing their abilities in specific areas (Dweck and Legget 1988; Molden and Dweck 2000). They believe that effort leads to increased ability.

Children's beliefs about intelligence not only influence their goal orientation but also facilitate or limit success in all academic subjects (Stipek and Gralinski 1996). Think of your own learning. In what areas do you see your ability or competence increasing with effort? Math? Chemistry? Gardening? Sports? All of them? In what areas do you attribute success or failure to your own capacity or ability—and see effort and perseverance as pointless? Now think of your goal orientation in these areas. Do you see learning as an end in itself, your goal being to improve and learn more (knowledge), or are you concerned about how you look in front of others (performance)?

Classroom context is the other crucial factor in students' goal orientation. The way we structure our classroom and the messages we send are a big influence on whether students adopt a knowledge or a performance goal (Ames 1992; Meece 1991; Pintrich 2000). What we say about the purpose of learning and the meaning of achievement, what we reward in a class, the kind of feedback we give, the way we group students, and the autonomy we give them all shape students' goals (Alderman 2008). When we encourage self-direction in our students rather than specify directions and anticipated results, convey the intrinsic value of learning and reading, and value effort, we are more likely to foster a knowledge or learning goal orientation. Figure 1–5 describes instructional behavior that fosters knowledge goals rather than performance ones. Also, in Chapter 5 I describe ways to approach vocabulary instruction with ELs that are guided by the knowledge goals. Examples of how to infuse vocabulary instruction with knowledge goals are discussed within the framework of CORI and USHER in middle school.

Figure 1–5. Instruction That Encourages Knowledge Goals*

Instructional Behavior	What This Looks Like
Provide opportunities for self-directed learning	▪ The teacher helps students evaluate their own work; once skills and strategies are developed, students have more opportunities for self-direction and evaluation. ▪ The teacher helps students use feedback on first drafts to revise and improve them. ▪ The teacher provides a way to track student improvement in tangible ways.
Emphasize the intrinsic value of learning	▪ The teacher helps students do extra work to improve their learning, detaching it from the grade. ▪ The teacher emphasizes that failure does not mean "dumb"; it is a gauge of how to improve. ▪ The teacher helps students see that the label *smart* is not associated with higher grades; it means seeking learning opportunities and benefiting from them. Applications of what is being learned are consistently held.
Provide opportunities for student collaboration	▪ The teacher assigns tasks and projects that require students to work effectively together and help one another. ▪ Tasks are structured with clear individual as well as group goals.
Emphasize incremental, malleable intelligence	▪ The teacher emphasizes effort and persistence as critical for improved ability. ▪ The teacher frequently discusses student progress in relation to effort.
Provide opportunities for students to develop knowledge and learn specific strategies	▪ Ability increases are attributed to knowledge and skills rather than "being smart." ▪ The teacher offers opportunities to develop depth of knowledge over time in all content areas.
Emphasize comparisons with students' own previous performance rather than comparisons with others' performance	▪ The teacher encourages students to compare their most recent grades to previous ones to see if they have improved. ▪ There is a clear link between grades and one's own accomplishments. ▪ Rewards are provided for individual accomplishments rather than in competitions with classmates.
Emphasize tracking students' own learning rather than comparing grades	▪ The teacher ensures that students are clear on the learning objectives and ways to achieve them. ▪ Grade comparisons are deemphasized.
Provide opportunities for students to improve their work over time; recognize improvement in assessments	▪ The teacher helps students become knowledgeable about learning strategies (e.g., comprehension strategies) and how these can help with their learning. ▪ Teacher feedback indicates skill development and strategy use.
Provide thematic units organized around core concepts or principles in a content domain	▪ The teacher helps students have a broad, organizational structure for their learning that includes key core concepts within a domain or discipline. In this way, the focus is on key ideas that can be learned over time and from different angles (e.g., specific animals' adaptation through various examples over time; immigration patterns, reasons, and trends). The emphasis in on learning in depth over time.

*Adapted from *Motivation for Achievement: Possibilities for Teaching and Learning*, 3rd ed., by M. K. Alderman (New York: Routledge, 2008).

Autonomy: Scaffolding Independent Decision-Making

Supporting students' autonomy by offering them the opportunity to make choices increases their intrinsic motivation to read (Gambrell et al. 1996; Sweet, Guthrie, and Ng 1998). This has direct implications for teacher-student relations and classroom practices. Choice doesn't foster student engagement in and of itself. Allowing students to choose books, tasks, peers to work with, and topics to read about is becoming common practice. However, many of us are not fully aware *why* offering student choices enhances their engagement and motivation. Student choice is rooted within the broader practice of fostering autonomous learning. The combination of autonomy support (acknowledging the importance of students' opinions and feelings, providing choice in relation to students' interests, explaining the relevance of class activities) and classroom structure (clear expectations, consistent and predictable responses, strategy adjustments) encourages children's motivation and academic engagement (Skinner and Belmont 1993).

My colleagues and I were delighted by Spanish-speaking ELs' perceptive response to autonomy-supporting literacy instruction as part of a life-science unit on animals' adaptations to their environment (Taboada, Kidd, and Tonks 2009). These struggling readers eloquently articulated how important choice was in their learning. Juan said that being able to choose what animal to read about as part of a life science unit "helped me learn more deeply." He also said he liked having a say about the order of the topics he read about. Prompted to think of a time when he had no opportunity for choice, he responded, "Social studies test! You had to read the paragraph [everyone was] reading." He felt "kind of bad" about this: "I want to learn about this paragraph, not that paragraph." He found the test boring because he couldn't choose what to read.

Struggling readers need choices as much as, or perhaps more, than stronger readers: "Lower achievers needed more choices in reading and writing situations to initiate and sustain their effort and attention. Lower achievers also needed more relevant activities connected to reading and writing, which enabled students to see the usefulness of literacy, to gain confidence in their abilities, and enhance their self-perceived competence" (Sweet, Guthrie, and Ng 1998, 219).

Perhaps you're thinking, "Choice sounds good, but how do I know what choices are better than others? How do I *choose* choices?" There can be so many options to choose from, and not every choice is meaningful for our students' learning. Although most of us think of choice in reading as letting students select their own books (a good thing), there are plenty of other choices we can offer that foster students' intrinsic motivation and reading engagement (see Figures 1–6 and 1–7).

Figure 1–6. A Menu of Choices for a Fourth-Grade Language Arts/Life Science Unit

CHOICE OF THE DAY	
4/28	My word for the word *log*
4/29	My question
4/30	My chart to show what I learned
5/1	My example about behavioral adaptations
5/2	My headings
5/7	My question word: Who, what, where, when, why, how
5/8	My partner/My reading buddy
5/12	My behavioral adaptations example
5/13	My level 3 question
5/14	My reading buddy/Level 3 question
5/15	My reading buddy
5/22	My info source: Glossary, dictionary, thesaurus, online, etc.

Figure 1–7. What Kinds of Choices?

Choice That Reflects Students' Interests and Goals

Choices should align with students' interests and personal goals and therefore nurture their sense of autonomous learning. In some cases, if choices align with students' cultural background they can foster a sense of relatedness to the school environment and to their peers.

Choice Scaffolded for Student Ability

Choice should develop students' sense of competence. Children are drawn to activities and books that engender a sense of competence—those at a comfortable level of difficulty or challenge (Sweet et al. 1998) or that they see as important to their learning (Cordova and Lepper 1996). For example, every third grader realizes that choosing what color pencil to use to complete today's homework assignment is less important than choosing what American colony to research for a final project.

Choice That Is Academically Relevant to Students' Learning and Achievement

For example:

- What type of graphic organizer to use to represent the ideas in a text
- What section of a book to read
- How to share new knowledge with one's peers (e.g., what type of culminating project)
- What text-based questions to ask (see Chapter 5)
- What partner to work with on partner reading
- What heading to give to a specific team project

Organizational choices (regarding classroom management, for example) and procedural choices (how they will demonstrate their knowledge) help students feel comfortable in the classroom, but their impact may be short-lived and fail to create deeper engagement in learning. Cognitive choices (tasks aligned with interests) foster more enduring student investment in deep-level thinking and academic engagement (Stefanou et al. 2004). In Chapter 5 I describe meaningful academic choices within the broader framework of autonomy-supportive learning. I do so keeping in mind the importance that this motivation practice has for struggling EL readers, and in relation to student text-based questioning, a comprehension strategy that lends itself well to provide students with a sense of control over their own learning and reading.

Collaboration: Reaching Beyond Ourselves for Meaning

Students need opportunities to work collaboratively in pairs or small groups on literacy activities that focus on building knowledge through reading (e.g., "read this material, answer the essential questions of the day, and discuss your answers"; "read this material and create a museum exhibit on westward expansion"). My definition of collaborative literacy activities is based on theories of cooperative learning: students work together in groups small enough that everybody can participate in the task (Cohen 1994). The task is clearly presented, and students work without my direct supervision (but with my guidance as necessary). Four criteria guide collaboration in small groups:

1. Students have to talk to one another to accomplish the task; they need to hear how others approach the task and exchange ideas.
2. The task must provide a question or problem that stimulates students to cooperate as they formulate, share, and compare ideas.
3. The task must be broad enough to ensure both individual and group accountability (Vaca, Lapp, and Fisher 2011).
4. Students may play various roles in completing the task (e.g., when creating a museum exhibit on western expansion, one student is the illustrator, another is the narrator, another is the tech expert, etc.).

Small-group collaboration on a reading activity has two purposes: students must learn something by reading a text *and* discuss what they've learned with one another. This social interaction around content helps students deepen their knowledge about a topic, develop expertise, and as a result become more interested and motivated. Think of something you're really interested in—cooking?

yoga? mountain climbing? You share and discuss this interest with others, ask their opinions about it, refine your ideas, seek more information, get excited. Discussing, comparing, contrasting, summarizing, and searching for information are more enjoyable in pairs or small groups than alone.

Sharing what one learns is motivating in and of itself. However, we need to establish a clear group objective, assign tasks clearly, and help students set specific individual goals within the group. Structure and accountability are essential for effective collaboration. Productive work in small groups involves conceptual learning and higher-order thinking (Cohen 1994). Conceptual learning is directly related to content; students need an interesting topic they can investigate in deep, conceptual ways. The meaningful discussions that arise contribute to the development of higher-order thinking (Noddings 1989). Figure 1–8 lists ways we can encourage students to collaborate effectively.

Figure 1–8. How to Help Students Collaborate

1. Create the conditions for effective collaboration.
   - Establish clear group rules and objectives, preferably with student input.
     » Allow every student to participate.
     » Establish what groups should do if a question comes up while you are working with another group.
     » Model appropriate group interactions (see Figure 7–9). You can also model ineffective group participation (e.g., students not taking turns to talk and listen to each other) so that students can see the contrast between effective and ineffective collaboration.
     » Encourage detailed or elaborate explanations, for you and within the group. This helps ELs become familiar with academic language.
     » Praise students for appropriate group interactions.
     » Assign specific roles within the group as appropriate.
   - Identify a task that requires collaboration.
     » Create or choose a task students cannot reasonably complete independently. Some researchers recommend presenting tasks in a way that requires discussion.
     » Include opportunities for students to revise or comment on one another's work.
   - Form groups that can successfully complete the task. (Consider the goal of the activity as well as students' strengths and weaknesses.)
     » Vary how groups are formed. Sometimes it's better to group students with similar skills or abilities. Other times, each group should have a mix of student skills and abilities.
     » Don't change groups during the activity unless absolutely necessary (e.g., behavior issues, a prolonged absence).
2. Provide students the materials and systems needed for successful collaboration.
   - A written copy of the rules or steps involved (e.g., directions for partner reading).
   - Clearly stated goals that allow students to contribute to one another's knowledge rather than duplicate their efforts.

(continues)

Figure 1–8.   How to Help Students Collaborate *(continued)*

- A system for distributing and collecting materials.
- If appropriate, a written copy of the various roles.
- Rewards if they encourage individual accountability (e.g., team scores [Cohen 1994]).

3. Monitor groups as they are working. (Don't micromanage [Cohen 1994]).

- When not working directly with one group:
  » Circulate through the room.
  » Listen to what students are saying.
  » Ask each group one or two quick questions to judge their progress or understanding.
  » Ask a question to redirect behavior or make them think about the material in a new way.

- When working with a group:
  » Be aware of how long you spend.
  » Give specific feedback.

4. Support ELs' language development.

- When feasible, present culturally relevant texts through a guided discussion connecting the content to students' lives. (See prompts for discussion in Chapter 6.)
- Encourage ELs with higher English oral proficiency to vocalize softly as they read the text (Avalos et al. 2007). This helps with fluency and pronunciation.
- Reinforce word recognition through morphological awareness* (Avalos et al. 2007). This develops word recognition and vocabulary skills.
- Use vocabulary journals or logs that link key content vocabulary to group activities (Avalos et al. 2007).

*Morphological awareness refers to understanding and using word parts that carry significance, such as root words, prefixes, and grammatical inflections (e.g., -s or -es for plurals; -ing, -tion endings). These word parts are morphemes—they can add to or change a word's meaning.

The amount of interaction within a small group depends on the nature of the task (Cohen 1994). Tasks that can be carried out by individual students or completed by specific responses do not promote true collaboration. True collaboration takes place when the tasks are open-ended (more than one response is feasible) and support a true mutual exchange of ideas among *all* students (above-, on-, and below-grade-level readers) in the group.

I use two forms of small-group work to foster collaboration: small group reading activities and unit final projects. In both, students read books that are either (1) different topics on different or similar reading levels (e.g., a different American Colony for each group member) or (2) at different reading levels on the same topic (e.g., reasons for the Civil War). The choice depends on the nature of the task. The goal of small-group reading activities is to hone students' reading and content knowledge on a topic that has been addressed in whole-class instruction. The goal of a unit final project is for students to apply already-learned or read material in creating a group product. Both require student collaboration, but each has a different way of guiding students to collaborate (reading more deeply on a topic for small group reading; applying newly learned knowledge for culminating projects). Detailed examples of small-group collaboration are provided in Chapter 7. As with other chapters, suggested ways to weave the motivation practice with a comprehension strategy are suggested. In this chapter I included comprehension monitoring, a versatile strategy that lends itself well to student collaboration in relation to literacy tasks. Student grouping recommendations are listed in Figure 1–9. The type of grouping depends on the type of task, your goals, and the type of interaction generated within the group.

Five motivation practices—self-efficacy, meaningful academic choice, relevance, mastery goals, and student collaboration—are shown to make a substantial improvement on student performance, specifically, supporting students engagement with literacy. These practices improve the performance of not just struggling readers but all readers (e.g., Guthrie, McRae, and Klauda 2007) including ELs (e.g., Taboada Barber et al. 2015). Of course, there is no one plan for how these practices should be implemented; you adapt based on your literacy materials and your students (and you'll see what that looks like in Chapters 3–8). In fact, differentiation is part of what makes these practices motivating: they are

Figure 1–9. Effective Grouping for Successful Collaboration on Literacy Tasks

- Keep groups flexible and regroup based on ongoing observation (Ash 2002).
- Allow students to work with students of all reading levels with similar interests *or* similar reading levels with different interests (Ash 2002).
- Use needs-based grouping some of the time: Keep groups to a maximum of six students (four is optimal) with similar strengths and instructional needs (Avalos et al. 2007).
- Use alternative grouping some of the time: Pair students with varying instructional needs. For example, pair a couple of students who struggle with word recognition but have high background knowledge on a topic with a couple of students with the inverse reading profile.
- Mixed Ability grouping: Remember that lower achievers benefit from working in cooperative groups with higher achievers, even when the tasks demand high-level thinking (Tudge 1990).
- Groups should meet three to five times a week for twenty or thirty minutes each time.
- Determine beforehand if ELs need to be paired/grouped with native speakers whom they can ask for reassurance or clarification.
- Be aware of status problems: recognize the importance of the various abilities students can contribute to the group (Hoffman 1973; Rosenholtz 1985).
- Suggest roles for each student that contribute to the group goal. If appropriate, make each student responsible for a different resource to contribute to the end product (Cohen 1994).
- Whenever possible, encourage students to specify goals for the group precisely, plan procedures, select alternatives, and modify their plans to achieve their goal (Chang and Wells 1987; Cohen 1994).

not inherent traits of every student, impervious to teacher influence. We must always remind ourselves that anything that is not inherent in every student requires our instruction. This is true not just for motivation, but also for behavior and content; for any expected outcome that is not uniformly met, there must be instruction. When we just focus on the cognitive dimensions of reading comprehension and do not offer ELs opportunities to thrive in each of these dimensions of motivation, we exclude them from essential components of engaged learning. Children will not all learn at the same pace and in the same way, but they can all learn. Without a clear understanding of what reading skills, content, and motivation practices will lead to learning from informational texts, we demotivate and deprive our ELs of opportunities to grow academically. However, if we purposefully teach motivation practices, we encourage ELs to build their belief in their own success as well as the skills they need to realize it.

2

Understanding How ELs Acquire
New Knowledge

Most elementary and middle school teachers are quite familiar with the teaching of comprehension strategies. We use the KWL charts, visualizing, semantic maps, or Question-Answer Relationships (QAR), and we know that teaching these strategies effectively has a positive effect on students' comprehension. However, when I talk with teachers I find there is less known about the reasons for comprehension strategies—the *why* we need to teach them—and *how* to teach them in ways that are particularly effective with ELs, who are not only struggling with reading but also developing their proficiency in English. In this chapter I hope to provide a bit more help with understanding which comprehension strategies are most effective with ELs. I introduce these strategies as they apply to informational texts: activating background knowledge, student text-based questioning, identification of main idea and comprehension monitoring. I also describe the teaching of vocabulary to ELs, which is better described as an instructional practice than a comprehension strategy, but it deserves special attention in light of ELs' struggles with academic vocabulary as they move up the grades. In Part 2 of this book we explore these strategies and practice in action.

When I refer to comprehension strategies I mean the cognitive tools or operations that readers engage in to comprehend text. So, although these are, and ought to be, explicitly taught by teachers, the ultimate goal is for students to apply them independently during their reading. In contrast, instructional practices comprise steps in which the teacher is primarily leading the action on how to perform an operation, such as an activity to assist students with academic or technical vocabulary words. In this sense this book includes four comprehension strategies, and vocabulary activities would, in their majority, fall into the category of instructional practices.

When we consider comprehension strategies, we must consider two important dimensions. One relates to their *intentionality* (Pressley and Harris 2006). Certainly, when we first learn to use a comprehension strategy we are quite intentional: we deliberately plan its use, when we are going to apply it, and how. As you teach from the strategies in this book, you will likely find yourself being very explicit in naming the purpose and practice of a strategy. However, with your students' increasing comfort and expertise, strategies that were initially quite deliberate become much more automatic, requiring less conscious attention (Pressley & Harris 2006). This leads us to the second dimension of comprehension strategies—their automaticity and *independent use*. This latter dimension relates to *how* you teach comprehension strategies (as well as student-led vocabulary learning skills) through the gradual release of responsibility model (GRR) (Pearson and Gallagher 1983) and to the importance of teaching ELs how to become active readers.

Why We Teach Comprehension Strategies

Comprehension strategies help students construct and integrate new knowledge. Research on these strategies came from work conducted on how good readers think during reading. Research conducted via think-alouds (Pressley and Afflerbach 1995) reveals that good readers interact with text in specific ways. They question what they read; they think of what they know and connect it to information in the text; they note conflicts between what they know and what they read; they make partial summaries as they read; they make predictions about upcoming text. Good readers also read selectively, depending on their purpose. These comprehension strategies should not be a privilege of good readers; they should be taught explicitly to all readers. "The case is very strong that teaching elementary, middle school, and high school students to use a repertoire of comprehension strategies increases their comprehension of text" (Pressley 2000, 5).

Many reading, language arts, and English teachers include teaching reading comprehension strategies in their curriculum. However, much of the reading to learn that students do happens in the content areas, and many content-area teachers do not feel qualified to provide (or do not feel responsible for providing) explicit instruction on reading comprehension (Greenleaf et al. 2001; Ness 2009). Teachers cite lack of instructional time and the pressure to cover content as barriers to comprehension strategy instruction (Bulgren et al. 2000; O'Brien, Stewart, and Moje 1995; Scanlon, Deschler, and Schumaker 1996). One study found that only 3 percent of class time was devoted to comprehension strategy instruction (Ness 2009) in science, geography, and history in grades 6 through 11, and strategy instruction for informational text is also uncommon at the elementary grades (Hall and Sabey 2007). These statistics became real to our research team when one of the seventh-grade social studies teachers in our first USHER professional development session asked, "Are you saying you would like me to have my students sit in small groups reading different things in the Growth of Industry unit? How am I supposed to follow what each one is doing and account for their learning if they are not all listening to the same information?!" The mere idea of having students read in small groups during history class was foreign to this teacher. You can imagine how that same teacher may have perceived the idea of teaching comprehension strategies as part of the social studies curriculum!

Even teachers who see comprehension strategy instruction as necessary may be unsure of the reasons. Why is it important to state the purpose of a strategy explicitly? Why match specific strategies with specific genres? Why use a comparative graph to understand similarities and differences between the arctic tundra and the boreal forest? Why use a Venn diagram to understand the collective economic, political, and social circumstances that led to the Civil War? These are all fair questions. They reveal a real need for strong models of comprehension strategy instruction for informational texts that often are neglected.

The adoption of the Common Core State Standards (CCSS) (National Governors Association Center for Best Practices, Council of Chief State School Officers 2010) means that teachers are expected to better integrate literacy with content. Some teachers mistakenly believe that strategy instruction distracts them from the content-area reading expected of them or from the CCSS. However, many of the CCSS call for strategy instruction; for example, CSS.ELA-Literacy. RI.4.1 and 4.2 require identification of details, main ideas, and references to explicit text information, all skills that require comprehension strategies; similarly, CSS.ELA-Literacy.R.I.6.5 requires analyses of how a particular sentence or paragraph fits into the overall structure of a text, which also requires strategies such as organizing graphically, identifying and prioritizing ideas, and summarizing. This integration of literacy and content is especially important for ELs.

Without comprehension instruction, EL's understanding and retention of content-specific information is limited (Alvermann 2001; Biancarosa and Snow 2006; Kamil 2003; Heller and Greenleaf 2007; Torgesen et al. 2007). With instruction, ELs' comprehension increases not only on standardized reading tests but also in content areas such as American history (Taboada et al. 2015). In my view this is because, in no small part, strategies help students dig deeper into the text and thus learn more from the text. If we coupled comprehension strategies with motivation supports—such as fostering relevance for history topics through explicit explanations or authentic reasons for reading—ELs' gains in content area reading are highly likely to improve.

The Power of Explicit Instruction

Good strategy instruction means explicit instruction on the use and purpose of strategies and scaffolded practice toward independence, also known as the gradual release of responsibility. In the gradual release of responsibility (GRR) (Pearson and Gallagher 1983), the teacher takes initial responsibility by modeling a strategy in use. She names the process of using that strategy so that students can then practice the strategy on their own with different texts. She then helps the student become progressively more independent so that her support in strategy use is no longer needed or only needed in certain contexts, like a more difficult text. Figure 2–1 is a revisited version of the GRR (Duke, Pearson, Strachan, and Billman 2011) that draws special attention to the need for explicit explanations of strategies—the why and how.

Teachers must first explicitly explain or describe comprehension strategies to students and help them practice these strategies before students are ready to use them on their own (Pearson and Gallagher 1983; Pressley 2000; Pressley and Harris 2006). If students are made aware of the purpose for using a specific strategy, and when and why it is needed, they are more likely to internalize these strategies and transfer them to new texts (Pressley and Harris 2006). Let's go over each of the components or steps in the model proposed by Duke et al. (2011) as shown in Figure 2–1. I use student text-based questioning (described in depth in Chapter 6), to describe the flow of the GRR steps; you may be aware that these steps can be applied to almost any comprehension strategy.

1. *An explicit description of the strategy and when and how it should be used.* This generally takes place in the context of whole-class instruction. In the lower elementary grades, students are sitting on the rug and following the teacher's explanation and read-aloud. In the upper elementary

Figure 2–1. An Adapted Version of the Gradual Release of Responsibility Model

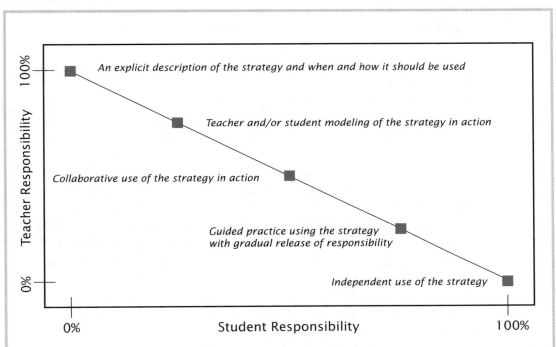

Source: "The Instruction of Reading Comprehension," by P.D. Pearson and M.C. Gallagher, 1983, *Contemporary Education Psychology, 8*(3), 317–344.

grades, most students are either seated in small groups or in other inter-active formats. The teacher's explicit description would be something like this: "Asking text-based questions is asking questions that come to mind before or during reading. You should ask questions as you read. For now, you should stop every one or two paragraphs that you read and ask a few questions. Asking questions helps with focusing our atten-tion and better understanding what we read."

2. *Teacher and/or student modeling of the strategy in action.* The class format for this step is also whole class, with students following the teacher's modeling: "I am going to ask questions while I read this paragraph. I will start with just the first paragraph here. Hmm . . . I see a picture of a frog. It looks like he—I think it is a he—is about to jump into a pond. I *wonder* how he is going to breathe once he is in the water. That is my question, I will write it down on a sticky note so I can go back to it later and answer it. . . ."

3. *Collaborative use of the strategy in action.* At this point students participate in the strategy with the teacher and apply it to the text together: "I have asked some good questions so far about frogs and their habitats. From this part on I want you to ask questions with me. Each of us should stop and think about a question we have for each paragraph or couple of sentences that we read. . . . Okay, now let's hear what your questions are."

4. *Guided practice using the strategy with gradual release of responsibility.* During guided practice, students can either be in a whole-class format applying the strategies in small pairs or groups, or they can do it individually. The difference with the previous step is that they are responding to the strategy in a more individual way. *Earlier:* "I have called Juan and Maria together to work on asking questions while you read the frog book and other books. After every few pages I will ask each of you to stop and ask a question. We will talk about your questions and then read on to see if we can answer them." *Later on:* "Each of you has a chart that lists different pages in your book. When you finish reading a page on the list, stop and check the questions you asked. Write the questions in the column that says 'My Questions.' When you get to the next page on the list, check off whether your question was answered or what level it was." (See Chapter 6 for question levels.)

5. *Independent use of the strategy.* Class format for independent use generally has a setting that allows for individual strategy use, whether this involves students working individually within small groups or in a more traditional classroom layout. "It is time for silent, individual reading. As you read today, remember what we have been working on asking questions while we read. Be sure to ask questions every one or two paragraphs. Ask yourself if your question was answered, and what level it was. Check as you read to see whether your question helped you understand the paragraph better. Maria will write one question per team on the classroom poster! We'll discuss answers later today!"

The GRR, if well implemented, shows metacognition in action. When a teacher explains the purpose of a strategy as part of her instruction, she provides "metacognitively rich" instruction (Pressley and Harris 2006). Metacognitively rich instruction is especially valuable for struggling readers in the middle grades; these students don't have a strong sense of themselves as readers, and the value of thinking about their thinking (i.e., metacognition) escapes them. Making struggling readers aware of the usefulness of strategies gives them an understanding of reading for meaning they may not have had before. ELs who have some oral English proficiency respond well to, and benefit from, explicit comprehension strategy instruction—questioning, making inferences, monitoring, summarizing, visualizing, and identifying the main idea (Proctor, Dalton, and Grisham 2007; Taboada and Rutherford 2011; Taboada et al. 2015; Taboada, Bianco, and Bowerman 2012; Jimenez 1997; Taboada, Kidd, and Tonks 2010).

Engagement Drives Strategy Use

As I discussed in Chapter 1, engagement is more than a "nice-to-have" side effect of good instruction. Student engagement in reading reflects deep comprehension. When students use comprehension strategies they become more engaged with the text and, vice versa, when a book piques their curiosity and interest they are likely to invest themselves cognitively and increase their strategy use (Guthrie et al. 1996). My colleagues and I found a strong association between sixth- and seventh-grade ELs' reading engagement and their use of comprehension strategies. Using Reading Engagement Index (REI) criteria (see Figure 2–2), teachers rated students' reading engagement three times during an eight-week period. We also assessed students' use of specific comprehension strategies—identifying the main idea and supporting details in short paragraphs and text-based questioning—and we asked them about their awareness (metacognition) of the importance of identifying relevant information. ELs weakest in their use of strategies were the least engaged; moderate strategy users were more engaged than the weakest strategy users; and the strongest strategy users were the most engaged (see Figure 2–3).

Marina, a sixth grader who struggled with using strategies with informational texts, often confused main ideas with supporting details and had a hard time conveying why finding relevant ideas in text helps understanding. She said, "Finding main ideas is important because we can tell the teacher what these are. We also know what to write for our group work." Marina's response indicates a disengaged reader—she reads exclusively for external reasons and finds main ideas so that she can tell her teacher, not because these help with her understanding of content. Marina's other behaviors indicated a clear lack of interest in reading both fiction and informational texts.

Anthony, who used strategies moderately well with informational texts, consistently identified main ideas in short paragraphs and asked higher-level questions (factual rather than yes/no) than did the weakest strategy users. However, he struggled with identifying supporting details and asking conceptual questions. When asked about the importance of identifying relevant ideas in text, he stated:

Figure 2–2. Reading Engagement Index

This Student	Student 1			Student 2			Student 3		
	NOT TRUE	**VERY TRUE**	**N/A**	**NOT TRUE**	**VERY TRUE**	**N/A**	**NOT TRUE**	**VERY TRUE**	**N/A**
1. Often reads independently.	1 2 3 4 5		1	1 2 3 4 5		1	1 2 3 4 5		1
2. Reads favorite topics and authors.	1 2 3 4 5		1	1 2 3 4 5		1	1 2 3 4 5		1
3. Is easily distracted in self-selected reading.	1 2 3 4 5		1	1 2 3 4 5		1	1 2 3 4 5		1
4. Works hard in reading.	1 2 3 4 5		1	1 2 3 4 5		1	1 2 3 4 5		1
5. Is a confident reader.	1 2 3 4 5		1	1 2 3 4 5		1	1 2 3 4 5		1
6. Uses comprehension strategies well.	1 2 3 4 5		1	1 2 3 4 5		1	1 2 3 4 5		1
7. Thinks deeply about the content of texts.	1 2 3 4 5		1	1 2 3 4 5		1	1 2 3 4 5		1
8. Enjoys discussing books with peers.	1 2 3 4 5		1	1 2 3 4 5		1	1 2 3 4 5		1

Source: Guthrie et al. 2004

Figure 2–3. Continuum of ELs' Strategy Use and Its Relation to Engagement

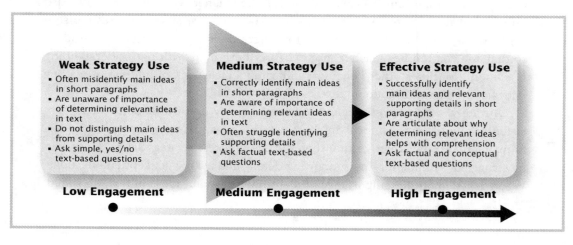

Weak Strategy Use
- Often misidentify main ideas in short paragraphs
- Are unaware of importance of determining relevant ideas in text
- Do not distinguish main ideas from supporting details
- Ask simple, yes/no text-based questions

Medium Strategy Use
- Correctly identify main ideas in short paragraphs
- Are aware of importance of determining relevant ideas in text
- Often struggle identifying supporting details
- Ask factual text-based questions

Effective Strategy Use
- Successfully identify main ideas and relevant supporting details in short paragraphs
- Are articulate about why determining relevant ideas helps with comprehension
- Ask factual and conceptual text-based questions

Low Engagement   **Medium Engagement**   **High Engagement**

"I think it is good to find important ideas in books because that way we can tell what is the message from the author or the important things to know." When asked how to distinguish main ideas from supporting details, he was off the mark: "Supporting details are things that you find in captions or next to the diagrams; they are not important to what you read." Anthony is clearly more invested in his reading than Marina, and as a result he can convey a clearer view of the main ideas and details than Marina can. For Anthony, main ideas are "the message from the author" rather than something to share with your teacher as Marina shares.

Sonia, who was quite flexible in her use of comprehension strategies with informational text, successfully identified main ideas and relevant supporting details in short paragraphs. She was also quite articulate about why determining relevant ideas helps comprehension: "If we cannot find what is important and what is not in a text or a book, then we are, like, flooded with information! We do not know what we really know or need to know! It feels too much. Finding main ideas help us with organizing our thinking." Sonia's response reflects a learner who uses the comprehension strategies with independence and for intrinsic reasons, a more engaged reader. If we effectively and persistently teach ELs comprehension strategies that they then integrate into their content-area reading, they feel more in control of their reading, more competent, and more engaged.

How We Acquire New Knowledge

As teachers, we understand the complexity of understanding and teaching comprehension. For at least three decades, cognitive psychologists have tried to explain the nature of comprehension. Comprehension depends on integrating new knowledge within a network of prior, or background, knowledge. New knowledge needs to stick to something. The notion of *network* is key. Schema theory proposes that knowledge is represented in nested categories rather than as isolated facts (Rumelhart 1984, 1994). We quickly activate our knowledge of train stations, for example, because it is clustered around a few big identifiable ideas; key characteristics of a train station (trains, tracks, ticket offices, a food court, signs), types (big, small, urban, rural), how they compare with other transportation centers, and so on (see Figure 2–4).

Each of us has a conceptual framework, based on what we already know, from which we build new understandings. When learners don't have experiences that prompt them to connect to what they already know, acquiring new knowledge is challenging. This is especially true with regard to reading informational texts in the upper grades, when texts become more complex and the main purpose is to learn and build knowledge. To understand what that feels like for our

Figure 2–4. Representation of Schema

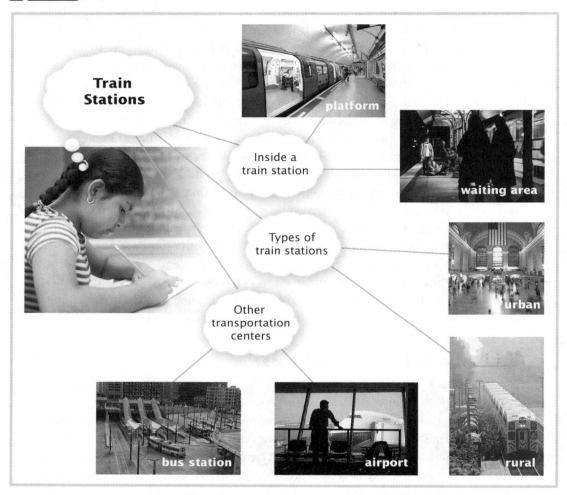

students, think about a topic that is not well organized in your mind. For example, I know very little about car engines. When reading material about car engines, I would need a lot of help in order to build a schema. I would probably need to learn more about the vocabulary and concepts discussed in the text. As teachers, an awareness of students' schema helps us scaffold our students from what they already know about a topic to what new understandings a text offers them. The right kind of reading instruction helps students correct misconceptions, organize knowledge that is disjointed, develop relevant content-area knowledge, and artic-ulate connections with their experiences.

What does that look like? When reading we *construct* knowledge by bringing some of our background knowledge to the act, and that knowledge is *integrated* with the new information we gain from text, changing our original body of knowledge. With this integrated knowledge we create mental representations of what the text means. Representations constructed during and/or after reading are integrated or fused with the knowledge stored in our mind (e.g., Kintsch 2004). Duke and her colleagues (2011) call this the virtuous (as opposed to vicious one) cycle of comprehension in which knowledge begets comprehension, which in turn begets new knowledge and is ultimately called *learning*. By truly comprehending, we literally know more than we did before (see Figure 2–5).

Figure 2–5.   Activating background knowledge and connecting it to text.

Before reading: What do I know about photosynthesis?

I know all living things need food. Human eat food; so do animals. What do plants eat? How do they find nutrition?

What is Photosynthesis?

Photosynthesis may sound like a big word, but it's actually pretty simple. You can divide it into two parts: "Photo" is the Greek word for "Light," and "synthesis," is the Greek word for "putting together," which explains what photosynthesis is. It is using light to put things together. You may have noticed that all animals and humans eat food, but plants don't eat anything. Photosynthesis is how plants eat. They use this process to make their own food. Since they don't have to move around to find food, plants stay in one place, since they can make their food anywhere as long as they have three things.

The three things are Carbon Dioxide, Water, and Light. You have probably heard of Carbon dioxide. It is a chemical that is in the air. Every time you breathe in, you breath in a bunch of chemicals in the air, including oxygen and carbon dioxide. Carbon dioxide is also one of the chemicals that causes global warming. But we'll get to that in a little bit. Here's what photosynthesis looks like:

Carbon Dioxide + Water + Light ----> Sugar + Oxygen

After reading: What do I know about photosynthesis?

Oh, I see! For plants, photosynthesis is sort of like my own eating because they eat sugar, too. Also they need light to make it useful for them. The difference with animals is that plants make their own food.

The comprehension strategies give ELs specific moves they can make when reading an informational text. Comprehension strategy instruction is motivating in and of itself because it specifies what children can do; it articulates specific responses to a difficult text beyond "I get it/I don't get it." Figure 2–6 articulates the comprehension strategies that matter most for ELs.

Activating Background Knowledge: What Do I Already Know?

Have you ever begun an activity by asking: "What do you know about the Civil War? Photosynthesis? Life in the ocean? Symbiosis in the animal kingdom?" Our students' blank looks may indicate that our expectations of what they should or could know are unrealistic. Triggering students' existing knowledge on a topic isn't always easy, but developing the habit of thinking about what we know about a topic and connecting it to our current reading is fundamental to understanding text.

Background knowledge is defined as knowledge gained from previous experience (National Reading Panel 2000)—material we've read, things we've done, or facts and concepts we've been taught. Ample research has shown that leading students to activate their background knowledge on a topic positively affects what they learn and remember (Anderson 1978; Anderson, Pichert, and Shirey 1983).

For ELs in particular, activating background knowledge often means helping them *build* a knowledge base before they read and then helping them *activate* that

Figure 2–6. Comprehension Strategies That Matter for ELs

Background Knowledge	What do ELs already know?
	How can they express it in English and/or their native language?
Vocabulary	What language is important to this topic?
	Are there additional words/concepts that would be helpful to ELs?
Main Idea(s) and Supporting Details	How do informational texts prioritize information?
Text-based Questions	How can questions help ELs locate their understanding of a text and deepen it (rather than seeing confusion as a deficit)?
Monitoring Comprehension	What in the text is confusing? Is the confusing language conceptual or text-based?
	How can ELs gauge what they know and address misunderstanding?

knowledge. Researchers have shown us that students who lack a relevant knowledge base do not comprehend text as well as students who do (Deshler, Ellis, and Lenz 1996; Goldman and Rakestraw 2000). Among these children are ELs who are new to English vocabulary and struggle with key concepts in specific disciplines (such as *atmosphere, photosynthesis*, and the *Underground Railroad*). Unless they are able to activate their background knowledge applicable to informational text in a cohesive way, they will at best recall isolated facts. If my car mechanic tells me my car needs oil, I understand. But if he starts talking to me about alternators, belts, brake rotors, and ball joints, I haven't a clue. This is how many ELs feel when asked to do a think-pair-share or complete a KWL chart.

Most relevant to texts typically read in schools, levels of background knowledge are also associated with socioeconomic status (SES). ELs and English native speakers of low SES have a harder time with oral and reading comprehension than ELs and native English speakers of higher SES (Hannon and McNally 1986). ELs in the United States who have gone to school and developed literacy skills in their first language are more inclined to respond well to strategy instruction, are more aware of which strategies can assist them with comprehension, and are more likely to have developed background knowledge to draw from (Jimenez 1997). Good EL readers can use their first language to their advantage by using specific strategies, such as cognates (i.e., words that share similar meanings or spellings across languages—condicion/condition, hospital/hospital, and temperatura/temperature are examples of Spanish-English cognates). Poor or struggling second-language readers are not necessarily aware of the benefits that speaking two languages can have for their reading (Jimenez 1997).

We can help struggling ELs by showing them that knowledge of concepts in one's first language provides a strong basis for learning the terms/words for these concepts in the second language (Moll and Gonzalez 1994). One way to do so would be to build background knowledge for key terms in English leveraging Spanish-speaking ELs' knowledge of those terms in Spanish; using the same titles in both languages can achieve that purpose. For example, when Sarah began her unit on animal adaptations with her fourth-grade English for Speakers of Other Languages (ESOL) self-contained class, she ensured that key concepts about adaptations (e.g., camouflage, respiration, survival) were represented and posted in her classroom in English and Spanish. Given that all but one of her fourth graders were Spanish speakers, seeing these words prominently displayed in Spanish was a great boost for starting discussions and activating their knowledge of key concepts. See Figure 2–7 for some suggestions of books that grade 4 science teachers used for this purpose.

Figure 2–7. Science books in Spanish to support concept learning in English.

	English Titles	Spanish Titles
Life Science	CELs Benchmark Education Publishing	Las Células Benchmark Education Publishing
	Do Penguins Get Frostbite? Scholastic Publishing	¿Se Congelan los Pingüinos? Scholastic Publishing
	Desert Giant Scholastic Publishing	El Gigante del Desierto Scholastic Publishing
Earth Science	Wild Weather: Lightning! Scholastic Publishing	Clima Borrascoso: ¡Relámpagos! Scholastic Publishing
	What Makes an Ocean Wave? Scholastic Publishing	¿Cómo se Forman las Olas? Scholastic Publishing
	Magic School Bus at the Waterworks Scholastic Publishing	El Autobús Mágico Viaja por el Agua Scholastic Publishing
	Magic School Bus and the Climate Change Scholastic Publishing	El Autobús Mágico y el Calentamiento Global Scholastic Publishing

But, you may ask, what about those ELs who do not have a tight network of background knowledge in their first language for a given topic or text? Well, for those students you will have to help them *build* background knowledge before they can activate it. That is, you will first have to determine if the student has true limited (or absent) knowledge of the topic, or if this is masked by his limited English proficiency. Assistance from the ESOL specialist or a native speaker of the EL's first language can help with an informal assessment on this. If you find out that ELs need to build some knowledge, you can do a number of things *before* tackling the target text: pre-teach key vocabulary (key concepts), or have a class discussion on the main ideas of the text, or walk them through an Anticipation Guide (as I show you in Chapter 3) and decide what areas need your explanation, or have them read a book on a topic they need to build background on. For example, before reading a book on tsunamis, students may benefit from reading a book on how waves are formed; or before reading about the American Constitution, students can read a text at their independent reading level on the Articles of the Confederation. Pre-reading texts such as these should provide some background to relate to the target text that they read with their classmates in class. Building integrated units on the same theme, as I discuss in more detail in Chapter 7, with multiple texts, videos, visits from experts, hands-on activities, and experiences that revolve around the same theme or topic, is an even more powerful way to help students continually build and activate background knowledge on a topic over time. You can also prompt students to bring knowledge they have from their life experiences. For example, when discussing the topic of religious or cultural celebrations, most students will be familiar at least with notions of their culture's celebrations. These are good ways to bring all of your students' experiences into the reading act without letting limited background knowledge relevant to a text be constructed as a deficit, but rather as a platform to build from before reading.

Text-Based Questioning: What Questions Can Help Me Focus My Reading on This Topic?

Asking text-related questions enhances students' comprehension (National Reading Panel 2000) and refers to students asking questions about the text at hand rather than answering teacher questions (e.g., Taboada and Guthrie 2004). Two seminal studies conducted more than two decades ago found that the kinds of questions fifth and sixth graders asked prior to studying a unit varied with their knowledge of the topic. If children already basically understood a topic, their questions were more conceptual—and therefore advanced their understanding—than if they didn't. Conceptual questions denote curiosity, puzzlement, skepticism, or knowledge-based speculation: "Can you make a new fossil fuel by mixing existing fossil fuels?" "How does fuel energize cars, boats, planes?" "Does fossil fuel affect the ozone layer?" Informational questions, on the other hand, tend to require yes or no answers: "Is steam a fossil fuel?" "Is heat a fossil fuel?" "Are some fuels alive?" (Scardamalia and Bereiter 1992). Children ask questions seeking basic information when they need it; they also show what they already know by asking questions that probe beyond the basics.

After discovering Scardamalia and Bereiter's findings I explored how fourth graders' text-based questions related to their reading comprehension, taking their prior knowledge of the topic into account (Taboada and Guthrie 2004). Students wrote down what they knew about specific topics in ecological science, spent ten minutes browsing a number of trade books dealing with ecological issues, and then wrote down any questions their browsing had triggered. My goal was to get children thinking so they could ask both conceptual and basic information questions—and they did. Students who asked conceptual rather than basic questions demonstrated greater comprehension. However, their questions didn't depend solely on their prior knowledge of the topic: just browsing the texts prompted probing, higher-level questions. I learned three important things: (1) It helps to teach students different types, or levels, of questions (a question hierarchy is included in Chapter 6); (2) prior knowledge of a topic prompts conceptual questions, but browsing texts can also get children's juices going and spark their curiosity; and (3) text-based questioning increases comprehension (some reasons are included in Figure 2–8). The message is evident: student-generated text-based questioning, in which students ask *self-initiated* questions about the text *before* and *during* reading to help them understand it, is a great way to get students hooked on reading! In Chapter 6 I share specific ways that have been successful in teaching struggling reader ELs and English monolinguals how to generate text-based questions of varying levels.

Identifying Main Idea(s) and Supporting Details: What Are the Essential Ideas and Details That Structure This Text?

One way of helping students locate their understanding through confusion is by identifying the main idea of a section of an informational text. Identifying main ideas is central to reading comprehension. Although readers may have different purposes for reading a text depending on their interests and the context, detecting a main idea is invariably involved in successful comprehension (van den Broek et al. 2003). Furthermore, successful identification of a text's main idea is an indication that readers have formed a coherent representation of it—that they can recall and learn from it (Dole et al. 1991). The ability to identify the main idea develops incrementally; students in lower grades have more difficulty than students in upper grades (van den Broek et al. 2003). However, even third graders can identify main ideas successfully, and it is reasonable to start teaching main idea identification in the early grades.

The title of a narrative book helps students determine the main idea (van den Broek et al. 2003). However, sometimes informational texts have many sections with titles that may not communicate the main idea. This can make these

Figure 2–8. Reasons Text-Based Questioning Increases Comprehension

- Students set personal goals for reading and are self-directed in their pursuit of knowledge.
- Generating questions fosters curiosity and interest; interest is directly related to comprehension.
- With student questions rather than assessment as the focus of instruction, the pressure of providing the "right answer" is removed. This is a particular relief for ELs, whose struggle to convey an idea in correct English sometimes distracts them from focusing on content.
- Whether factual or conceptual, questions help students think about the topic and text more deeply.

texts more challenging. When asked to highlight the main idea, many struggling readers highlight every sentence, unable to distinguish what is interesting from what is important. Researchers have repeatedly found that elementary and middle school students struggle to identify main ideas within an informational passage (Baumann 1982, 1983; Dunn, Mathews, and Bieger 1979; Taylor 1980). Insufficient background knowledge may be a factor (Sjostrom et al. 1984). Struggling readers may also find a statement important to them when it is not the most important idea from the author's perspective. In both cases students do not have enough tools for the task.

Identifying main ideas needs to be taught, especially to struggling readers and ELs. Researchers have shown that main idea instruction improves comprehension of informational texts (Slavin et al. 2009; Sjostrom and Hare 1984). Knowing what to pay attention to and what to ignore, being flexible depending on the type of text, being aware of text structures and the author's purpose, and activating what one knows about a topic all play key roles in determining importance and main ideas.

Because standardized tests often ask students to identify the main idea as an isolated task, teachers often teach this strategy in isolation. Initially, teaching and learning the strategy on its own provides the practice students need to feel comfortable, and knowing how to apply the strategy in isolation gives students confidence and helps them understand its purpose. However, to improve overall reading comprehension and achievement students need to use strategies *flexibly* (Wilkinson and Son 2011; Pressley et al. 1992; Brown et al. 1996); they must not only use the strategies but also know *when* to use them. In Chapter 5 I discuss specific ways to teach identification of main idea and establishing relevance for informational texts.

Vocabulary: What Language Is Important to This Topic?

When we discuss schema and background knowledge, we sometimes make the mistake of equalizing student vocabularies with their background knowledge. But to build integrated schema we do not need all the words/vocabulary that go with each idea. Some ideas may not be refined enough and thus lack a label to go with them (for example, in my schema of dry cleaners, I may have the idea of large press irons, but I may not know what these are called or know all of their functions). ELs may have the concepts and not the words or labels for many ideas and still have more-than-rudimentary schema for several concepts. Yet words are crucial for comprehension.

The connections between vocabulary and comprehension, discussed in more detail in Chapter 4, have been well established in many research studies, some of which date to the early twentieth century. Educational psychologists and literacy researchers have repeatedly concluded that understanding the meaning of words is one, though not the *only*, prerequisite for readers to understand the overall text. Reading comprehension consists of several components, with a reader's ability to understand and remember word meanings as one of the most prominent (Anderson and Freebody 1981; Davis 1968; Rosenshine 1980; Thorndike 1917). Among second language learning research, some view learners making progress in language acquisition when new learning is communicated in a slightly more advanced syntactical structure than the learner's current competence (Krashen 1985). For example, if a student asks "Is day cold today?" a slightly more advanced syntactical form for this question could be "Is the weather cold today?" or "Is it cold today?" For ELs, this principle relates to teachers being aware of where students are in a continuum of language proficiency (like the WIDA Performance levels from Chapter 1) while also supporting extended independent reading (Krashen 1989; 2004). When students read deeply and widely within and across topics, they will be exposed to more words and will increase their vocabulary and language structures. Vocabulary is more than a consequence of one's general conceptual knowledge; it is built through broad reading. One feeds the other.

However, definitional knowledge or contextual knowledge (from wide reading) of a word are not always sufficient. Knowing a word requires a combination of different types of knowledge: its definition, its relationships to other words in a sentence or a paragraph, its varied meanings in various contexts, and often its components (such as prefixes and suffixes) (Nagy and Scott 2000; Stahl 1999). This complex knowledge develops over time. For example, a kindergartner may know the meaning of *crane* as the object used to lift heavy things, such as vehicles that he saw in a vocabulary big book. The same student as a first grader could learn the meaning of *crane* as the bird that flies over chimneys in stories. Later on she may learn the meaning of the same word in the sentence, "She had to *crane* her neck to see the child in the crowd." The awareness that the same word has not only multiple meanings but also more than one function—noun, verb—requires multiple exposures to the word over time in various contexts but awareness of these variations as well. This knowledge requires time and language development. As mature readers, what we do when we encounter an unknown word depends on whether we can understand the sentence without knowing the word, whether we are reading for enjoyment or reading to learn, and/or whether we have a dictionary handy and are inclined to look up the word. We also know that what we understand depends on our knowledge of the topic as much as of the words being used. If we love gardening and have read a lot about it, we probably won't be derailed by terms such as *alkaline soil, bolting, horticulture, germinate,* or *genus* because we have a deep background knowledge that allows us to connect new words to many different related ideas. However, these words may stop a gardening novice cold.

Good readers acquire much of their vocabulary through encountering unfamiliar words while reading (Sternberg 1987), but struggling readers cannot rely exclusively on learning words through wide reading. They read less than skilled readers and encounter fewer, mostly common words and as a result have more impoverished vocabularies (Stanovich 1986). Although an EL's vocabulary increases more rapidly in relation to base vocabulary than a native English speaker does, ELs will not catch up to their peers without specific, explicit vocabulary instruction (Beck, McKeown, and Kucan 2013; Kieffer and Lesaux 2012). Yet, because of the large number of words students have to learn within each discipline in the middle grades, relying exclusively on explicit vocabulary instruction is not sufficient. One of the ways we can best support vocabulary development is to encourage wide reading of appropriately challenging texts (Beck et al. 2013; Nagy, Herman, and Anderson 1985; Stahl and Nagy 2006) while helping students develop their own strategies for vocabulary learning. I discuss some of these vocabulary practices and self-learning straetegies in Chapter 4.

Comprehension Monitoring: What in the Text Is Confusing Me?

Comprehension monitoring is being aware, during and after reading, whether a text makes sense. Good readers have this ability; they know when they need to exert more effort to make sense of a text (Pressley 2000). They are aware when a word they have sounded out does not make sense in the context of a sentence or paragraph, and they also know when words within a sentence do not make sense syntactically. In a classic experiment, researchers found that fourth graders who were good comprehenders easily detected misused words within a sentence (*the boys* prayed *the teacher*) but poor comprehenders did not detect semantic or syntactic violations as easily (Isakson and Miller 1976). Literacy researchers long ago developed ways to teach children how to seek clarification when they do not understand what they read. Rereading is an important one (Palincsar and Brown

1984), but ELs can also be taught metacognitive tools such as thinking aloud to monitor their comprehension (Fitzgerald 1995).

As they read, students need to self-monitor, asking, "Is what I am reading making sense?" ELs need to be taught this explicitly. At a minimum, they "can try sounding out a puzzling word again or rereading the part of a text that seems confusing" (Pressley 2000). But more than that, ELs need to be taught to think metacognitively—to monitor whether they are truly understanding and decide whether and how to take compensatory action (Cassanave 1988). This does not mean that we hold ELs, or any student, to an expectation that they should be able to solve all confusion on their own; rather, that we teach them to respond to it, not to take it as a given, but to figure out how to access resources, be it strategies or teachers support, to address their comprehension challenges and grow from them. In Chapter 7 I provide specific ideas on how to model, scaffold, and guide ELs to independently monitor their comprehension during reading.

Remembering What ELs Need to Make Sense of Informational Texts

Sometimes we attribute ELs' challenges with comprehension to limited vocabulary knowledge. While it is true that ELs fall significantly behind their English native-speaking peers in vocabulary and that this gap is even more pronounced as they move through the upper elementary and middle school grades, reading comprehension encompasses other processes such as activating relevant background knowledge, integrating meaning across sentences, and making inferences that are not limited to word meaning. In other words, when we only focus on building vocabulary, we don't address other needs of our ELs. Using specific comprehension strategies can go a long way in helping ELs circumvent these comprehension challenges. When we help ELs see that texts can become more understandable by using specific strategies, we let them know that they're part of a community of readers in our classroom; their challenges are not unique to them or their language status since many native English speakers face the same challenges. This reality is important to communicate to ELs. We don't want them to see their language background as a limitation. Instead, we want to show them what strategies they can use to become successful readers of content-area texts.

PART 2

Instruction in Action

Models for Motivation and Comprehension of Informational Texts

Background Knowledge and Self-Efficacy

Feeling Competent About What I Know and Can Do

Melissa, a fifth grader in Vanessa Shann's science classroom, was asked to describe herself as a reader. Her initial response was, "I am not a good reader. I stumble over my words when I read aloud. I like reading silently sometimes, but I am not sure if I always understand." Unfortunately, Melissa's negative self-perception as a reader is not uncommon among ELs. Many describe themselves as "bad readers" and yet cannot explain what specifically goes wrong or is challenging for them. They just know they are struggling.

Effective and purposeful teaching can disrupt that sense of incompetence and self-doubt. When teacher Vanessa Shann focused on fostering Melissa's reading self-efficacy, Melissa had a very different perception of herself as a reader after only four weeks: "I am good at finding the main idea in short paragraphs, and I can also think ahead of what I know or do not, before reading—especially if it's a topic I like, like butterflies and bees! I am also good at asking good, challenging questions about insects and then finding the answers. But I do not like sounding out long words . . . I struggle with those. I guess I still need to practice those more." Melissa's new perception of herself as a reader is not the result of feel-good, empty praise. What it does reflect is that Melissa has been taught the specific actions that will improve her capability and competence or self-efficacy as a reader.

Vanessa identified specific behaviors and thoughts of a good reader. She modeled the actions and then provided scaffolded support toward independence and plenty of opportunities to practice across a variety of tasks and texts. She gave students specific focused feedback on each action, helping them recognize how they were succeeding and where they needed to focus to get better. We observe that thoughtful instruction is reflected in Melissa's precise statements about her use of different comprehension strategies. Perhaps the most exciting aspect of Melissa's statement is her shift from a fixed mindset about her capability as a reader—that it can't be changed—to an open one. She knows that she can improve and sets specific goals to do so. This chapter shows you excerpts from Vanessa's lessons to illustrate some of the practices that activated background knowledge that helped Melissa transform this mindset. When a teacher demonstrates that mistakes are information about how to get better, not a fixed definition of our personal deficits, students improve. Students who do not fear making mistakes are more likely to show effort and persistence (Perry, Chipperfield, Hladkyj, Pekrun and Hamm 2014). Thanks to Vanessa's instruction, Melissa is now this kind of student.

Activating Background Knowledge Deepens ELs' Literacy Competencies

In classrooms all across the country, teaching background knowledge is sometimes sacrificed due to perceived pressure of the Common Core State Standards (CCSS). The high expectations of CCSS for reading, especially content-area or disciplinary reading, has meant that many teachers have overemphasized the role of "close reading" at the expense of background knowledge. As a result, students miss an opportunity to integrate new knowledge from a text with what they already know. A narrow, close reading exercise may mean that students are "reading" an informational text but that student comprehension is probably not deep or lasting. Certainly, close reading skills have value. For example, students need to be able to find the main ideas and details of a text and justify their selection based on information in the text. However, for struggling readers, and for ELs in particular, who often lack foundational knowledge in the content domains, reading experiences need to focus on building and activating background knowledge. In fact, background knowledge activation and close reading are necessary and complementary tools. I have heard the argument that ELs do not have the necessary background knowledge to lead an Activating Background Knowledge (ABK) activity. However, limited background knowledge relevant to a given text argues for more time spent on building knowledge and connecting to what students already know. Limited background knowledge relevant to a given text means that readers are less likely to make the inferences required to integrate information in a text into coherent knowledge representations. Without thoughtfully scaffolded experiences activating background knowledge, these struggling readers have a hard time understanding that ". . . comprehending is like completing a jigsaw puzzle: all of the information must be used, the information must fit into place without forcing, all of the important slots must contain information and the completed interpretation must make sense" (Anderson and Pearson 1984, 68). To build background knowledge, we need to show students how to identify the existing architecture of their understanding. ABK needs to be taught and practiced in every content area classroom.

Using the Gradual Release of Responsibility Model for Instruction

This kind of instruction is best when taken in clear and purposeful steps. We call this phased-out instruction the gradual release of responsibility (GRR). As explained in Chapter 2, the GRR is the consistent use of a cycle of explicit explanation, modeling, guided practice with corrective feedback, and independent use and application that leads to effective and independent strategy use ((Pearson and Gallagher 1983), see Chapter 2 for a more complete explanation.) Starting comprehension instruction with the strategy of activating background knowledge using the GRR is particularly effective. Through this strategy students come to see that they bring knowledge to the reading experience. They can add and revise to knowledge that is already of value, but the student has to learn first how to identify what they know and how to evaluate what they know against new information in a text. This requires substantial scaffolding so that students can separate opinion from fact and levels of expertise and accuracy. Over time, the responsibility shifts from teacher demonstration and support to student independence. In this way, the student understands that each reading experience asks her to consider what new understandings are being offered. As you will see, Vanessa's instruction models this process as it plays out across time—it was not a one-shot lesson.

Explain Purpose

Vanessa knows that before she activates her students' background knowledge she must first explain why it is a worthy activity. By being explicit, she creates relevance and builds academic language in relation to the strategy. Using terms such as "background" and "activation" also provides English labels that ELs may have in their L1 (first language) as part of their L1 lexicon but not in English. This is especially useful with informational texts. Vanessa illustrates this strategy as she introduces the concept of activating background knowledge to her fifth graders using the GRR:

1. *An explicit description of the strategy and when and how it should be used.* "The human brain holds information, just like file folders do. When we learn or read something new about a topic, we relate it to what we already know about that topic, just like we put papers that belong together in the same file or folder. *Relating* new knowledge from text to what we already know helps us understand what we read better. Today I will show you a few ways we can *activate* what you know about a topic."

When Vanessa set the purpose for using ABK with her students, she showed them a file folder with "Insect Societies" written on it and explained that they would be adding to this folder in their brain. She told her students that brains file information like a folder system and when they learn and read something new it is helpful to connect it to something they already know. Because students would be reading informational texts on insect societies, she focused their attention on text features as a way to activate background knowledge. She posted the following explanation on chart paper so that students could easily reference it during their reading time.

"ABK: Readers recall what they know about the topic of a text before and during reading. The use of text features (captions, headings, bolded words, diagrams, etc.) can be good anchors for readers to activate what you already know before reading a book or section of it."

Students now have a clear reminder of why to use ABK and a concrete way of going about it.

Modeling the Strategy and Collaborating with Students

Once purpose is established, the teacher then plans a way to model that strategy in use. The model should provide students with information about the ways in which a skilled reader, writer, or thinker processes information. Modeling is almost always done with the whole class and typically lasts fifteen minutes or less. Most often this is done through a think-aloud (Kucan and Beck 1997). In a think-aloud, the teacher explains her thinking while reading. She shows the students the moves that they can follow. For example, when first introducing activation of background knowledge, students hear how she uses text features—pictures, diagrams, maps, or time lines—to help her identify what she knows about the topic.

Text features offer a way of activating knowledge that is directly related to the text, rather than tangentially (as often happens when we just invite students to "share what you know about such-and-such"). The use of text features to activate background knowledge does not preclude students bringing misconceptions to their reading, but that is okay. Readers comprehend by bringing their own schema about the topic of the text, not someone else's. ELs can benefit enormously from watching their teacher model a comprehension strategy, learning not only explicit good reading behaviors but also reading-related oral language. Again, ELs are expanding their linguistic knowledge by having an explicit model of how to ABK. The labels used for several text features—such as ToC, Glossary, Index, Captions, Diagrams—are across-content academic terms that not only help ELs through the process of ABK, but also expand their academic language repertoire. In other words, ELs benefit from explicit instruction of ABK by expanding their linguistic as well as their conceptual knowledge. Acquiring new labels associated with the steps involved in ABK expands linguistic knowledge; conceptual knowledge emerges from the possible links that are established among their prior knowledge and the text at hand. Figure 3–1 shows the guidelines for modeling ABK for informational text.

Later on, as her ELs develop English proficiency, Vanessa can model and scaffold the use of text features with language that is a bit more complex. For example, toward week three of the unit, Vanessa used a book titled *Insect Societies* (Green 2002) to teach the concept of social insects. The book had plenty of text features and captions that could elicit background knowledge at multiple levels. One of the captions read "Lonely Lives," which led Vanessa to model the use of text features for ABK like this:

> *"Look at the caption titled 'Lonely Lives.' I wonder whether the butterflies in the picture prefer to live alone. How would that be different from other butterflies that we've read about? Let's make a note of this."*

Later in the book, when reading the caption "Royal Emblem," Vanessa chimed:

> *"I see a crown in the illustration. I wonder whether there is a connection between bees and royalty, such as kings and queens. What does this make*

Figure 3–1. Guidelines for Modeling ABK for Informational Text

- **Remember that modeling is showing (not just telling)!** The goal of modeling is to show your thinking to students. Modeling consists of a (teacher) think-aloud to demonstrate the use of the strategy.
- **Timing is everything.** Modeling should not last more than twelve/fifteen minutes in any given lesson. The goal is to show your thinking while reading (i.e., the use of the strategy) in an explicit way. If you limit modeling to twelve minutes, this will allow students time for guided practice without losing their attention to the process.
- **Put attention on the text.** Either distribute a copy of the text to each student or project the sections/pages that you'll use for ABK on the board.
- **Do a think-aloud through text features.** Point out the different features: headings, subheadings, captions, chapters, pictures, diagrams, the index, the glossary, and special vocabulary (e.g., bolded).
- **Share two or three examples of your own ABK during the think-aloud.** Connect your own background knowledge to these specific text features. If possible, connect your knowledge to shared experiences, such as class field trips, so that you are modeling activating your own background knowledge as well as helping students connect to their own.
- **Reveal the C.H.I.P.S. poster (see Figure 3–2).** State how text features are helpful for ABK (i.e., they act as memory triggers to make us think of what we know and what we may want to learn about a topic).
- **Conclude your modeling with a reminder.** Talk again with students about the purpose for activating background knowledge.

you think of? Do you see any connections between these ideas and what we observed bees doing in their hive?"

With the use of these captions Vanessa is teaching her ELs how book authors use figurative language at times, and how that language is meant to draw us into the book, to call our attention. She is also able to have students make connections with their prior knowledge in more specific ways than earlier in the unit, because her students have been building knowledge on insects' lives for three weeks now. The activation of background knowledge should be ongoing until students learn to do it on their own. This is evident when students, before delving into a book, look at the cover, ask questions, and recall something they know about a topic; or, when looking at a title, make a prediction of what that section is going to be about. They are actively interested in the content of a text before reading it and during reading it!

But even when students can use the strategy independently, each of these steps may need to be revised as texts become more complex. Increasing the text and language complexity for doing so via text features is something teachers can think of as they move along within a unit or within strategy instruction. Take a look at how this works with the next step of the GRR, when teachers and students apply ABK together:

> *"I have used some text features to show you how to activate your BK for some topics in this book. Now, I want you to use other text features with me in other sections of this book. Each of us should stop and think about a text feature and what it makes us think of. . . . Okay, now let's hear what you know about these topics and what connections you are making."*

Leo shared how he used part of the book title, *Life Cycle,* on the cover to think about the full life of the monarch: "When I saw that title I thought we would learn about her life. How she lived from birth until she died." Similarly, Melissa chimed in to share that she had read three captions and looked at the illustrations in the first few pages of the book: "They helped me think of what else I wanted to know. I did not know what words like *chrysalis* and *larva* meant and the pictures helped me. I wondered how they [monarch butterflies] can be so strong and fly so far, when they are adults if they come from such little pouches when they are babies!"

Having effective models of how to use text features to simply think of what we know, or would like to know, about content is a great way to help students activate what they know about a topic and keep the content somewhat limited to the topic or text. Ultimately, the goal of ABK is to enhance comprehension by linking what a reader knows about a topic to the new knowledge or experiences he will build or gain from text. If students have clear parameters for eliciting this knowledge, they will likely be more effective in activating knowledge pertinent to the topic at hand, and thus link it to new knowledge in effective ways.

Guided Practice

Guided practice provides a time for students to put into practice what the teacher had previously modeled for them. It also provides a space for the teacher to assess students' understanding of the purpose and process of strategy use and decide whether further modeling is needed, or whether students can move into more independent application of the strategy. Guided practice activities can be defined as either individual, whole class, or small groups. The defining characteristics of guided practice are that teachers work through examples of applying strategies with the students and provide corrective feedback on the use of the strategy (Pearson and Gallagher 1983). See Figure 3–2 for guidelines for guided practice. A blank template is also provided in Figure 3–3.

Figure 3–2. Guidelines for Guided Practice of ABK

- **Remember!** Guided practice aims to provide time for students to apply a strategy (or strategies) with support from the teacher.
- **Structure background knowledge activation.** Distribute texts that lend themselves to using text features for ABK. Use a tool such as the C.H.I.P.S. handout so students have a guide to ABK via use of text features.
- **Discuss any other text features.** This includes those not included in C.H.I.P.S. that may help students with ABK. Ensure that students spend a few minutes browsing the text and discussing/sharing their background knowledge with a peer.
- **Take notes.** Allow students about five minutes to fill in their C.H.I.P.S. handout.
- **Share your knowledge and clarify misconceptions.** Redirect students' attention to the whole class and have students share a piece of information from their handout.
  » Be sure to have students identify which text feature helped them ABK.
  » Clarify misconceptions about the topic. That is, do not let students' misconceptions or vague links among features and knowledge go unattended; otherwise, these can be stored as appropriate. There is nothing wrong with probing, "What do you mean that the diagram showing photosynthesis made you think of your own eating?" When in doubt, probe and clarify!

Book title: Native Americans

C Chapter Title	What is the chapter title? What did the title remind you of? That the first Americans were before Christopher Columbus and his men came.
H Headings	What did the headings remind you of?
I Index	What words in the index make you think of something you already know?
P Pictures, Maps, Graphs, Images	What pictures, maps, graphs, or other images caught your attention? Why? That the Native American hunting buffalo on the great plains
S Special Vocabulary	What special vocabulary do you notice?

American Indians, Lessons 2-3

An EL student activates his background knowledge using C.H.I.P.S. before reading *Native Americans* by J. Cipriano.

Figure 3–3. C.H.I.P.S. Handout

C Chapter Title	What is the chapter title? What did the title remind you of?
H Headings	What did the headings remind you of?
I Index	What words in the index or table of contents make you think of something you already know?
P Pictures, Maps, Graphs, Images	What pictures, maps, graphs, or other images caught your attention? Why?
S Special Vocabulary	What special vocabulary do you notice?

Vanessa illustrates this step in this section of the lesson. After she has modeled the process with different text levels and helped students collaborate in using the strategy together, Vanessa will lead her students through this guided practice with gradual release of responsibility. Eventually, students will have learned to ABK on their own. In this snapshot, we see her using this model with Melissa:

Guided practice using the strategy with gradual release of responsibility: "Earlier I asked Melissa to show me how specific text features helped her think about what she knew about the monarch butterfly. Melissa shared that she used captions and illustrations to think of what she knew about monarchs as well as what she wanted to know more about. Remember Melissa wondering about how monarchs could become such long-distance migrants given how small they were when they were babies? Clearly, Melissa is thinking about this topic in depth, and those captions and pictures are helping her with her thinking. Melissa is using text features to activate her thinking, her knowledge on the topic of this book.

After every few pages I will ask each of you to stop and, first, identify two text features and then, tell me what they make you think of and what connections you are making to the text at hand. We will talk about your BK and then read to see how it relates or connects to the information in the book."

Later on: "Each of you has a chart that lists different text features, called C.H.I.P.S. When you finish reading a couple of pages, stop and write down what text features you used and what they reminded or made you think of."

Vanessa continued her students' guided practice by asking them to pull the book *Insect Societies* from their baskets in their small groups. Vanessa reminded them: "As we've been discussing, there are lots of good reasons to think about what we know before we read a paragraph, a page, or a book. Yesterday we observed bees' behavior on a video and in our school backyard. We took lots of notes on what we saw them doing, including how they helped each other. I'd like you to bring those notes back and also to look at some of the text features that we discussed yesterday and are listed on the board. Sometimes when I'm trying to think about what I know about a topic I do not know where to start. So using an aid such as C.H.I.P.S. helps me focus my thinking.

I'd like you to look at your C.H.I.P.S. handout and use it to go through text features. What do these features make you think of. What is it that you know about these topics? Then discuss what the text features make you think of and share your knowledge with a partner."

Guided practice also asks students to extend their thinking to another text. When using text features to activate background knowledge, the teacher asks students to share their background knowledge and explain which text features spurred their thinking. This type of guided practice is especially important for ELs who may need extra time to think through what they know. It also gives them an opportunity to link relevant schema to text. Since this step is so important, it is equally important for the teacher to provide specific, focused feedback to students on the process of background knowledge activation: Have they used text features? Have they brought up topics related to the text at hand? If some, or most, students bring irrelevant background knowledge, this is the time to correct misconceptions and bring students back to the topics at hand.

Independent Use of the Strategy

Once students are consistently answering teacher questions and requests for applying the strategy under guided practice, they are ready to start applying the strategy on their own. The key to independent practice is to give students the opportunity to transfer their learning/use of strategies to new topics and books. That is, independent strategy use is a way to solidify their understanding while becoming active readers (Frey and Fisher 2006). The key words here are *transfer* and *solidify* understandings—independent practice should meet the goals of a lesson and be directly related to guided practice, not the application of something new! Some teachers make the mistake of practicing a related or similar skill during independent practice instead of the exact same skill taught. For example, asking students to use an anticipation guide is another way to ABK; however, this activity is not the same as using text features for ABK. Many students, especially ELs, may struggle with the questions and language in an anticipation guide unless this has been modeled and practiced under guided practice. It is okay and necessary to use new texts for independent practice, but is essential to scaffold student learning by having students apply the same strategy or skill learned earlier. Pay attention to how Vanessa links the independent application of her lesson to the use of text features she modeled and practiced with her students. She ensures that during independent practice her students work toward automaticity of the strategy.

"It is time for silent reading. As you read today, remember that we have been working on activating what we know about a topic or topics before we read so we can connect it to what we read. Be sure to identify text features and use them for ABK. Write down your connections on the C.H.I.P.S. handout. Read a few pages. Check to see if your connection relates to what you read to see whether ABK helped you understand the text better!"

As students work independently, in small groups or alone, Vanessa moved around the room to assess whether more modeling of ABK was necessary during the next unit or lesson as well as providing specific, focused feedback. For example, when Melissa was using chapter titles and headings and annotating her thinking in C.H.I.P.S., she was copying the headings and the first sentence of each paragraph. Vanessa reminded Melissa that the goal here was to read the headings and then stop to think about what those headings reminded her of, if anything, but not to copy information from the book: "Think of what the purpose of using text features such as captions or headings is—thinking of what we already know. They are a tool to activate our knowledge, to remind us of what we may know about a topic, right? If, however, you write down what the text says but do not stop to think of what you may recall or know about a topic, you are skipping an important step before reading. . . ." Figure 3–4 includes some tips on how to scaffold your students' use of text features for ABK. Remember that the goal is to provide enough scaffolding so that students succeed in applying the strategy of ABK on their own.

Figure 3–4. Scaffolding Students Toward Independent Use of Text Features to ABK

- Remind students why it is important to activate background knowledge (enhances comprehension, increases relevance and recall of information, helps integrate knowledge across texts and topics).
- As students look at text features or complete an anticipation guide, you may want to stop after a few minutes and correct any misconceptions or provide a few tips to guide them in activating relevant content to the text.
- Once students start reading, depending on the key guiding questions of a unit and the content read so far, you may want to stop after a few paragraphs and ask students what they recall learning about the content. Talking about their prior knowledge helps them understand the units or lesson-guiding questions.
- If students are struggling with activating relevant background knowledge, give them examples by doing a mini-modeling lesson and demonstrating how your background knowledge links to the ideas in text.

Other Techniques to Activate Background Knowledge

There are many other ways to activate background knowledge, and it's worthwhile to explore all of them in your classroom, as different techniques work best in different contexts.

1. **Read-alouds.** "I read aloud sections of texts to spur discussion on specific topics before they conduct their own reading. Picture books, magazine/newspaper clips, or short informational passages help with this purpose." (Sarah, fourth-grade language arts teacher)

2. **Realia/visual aids.** "With my ELs, when possible, I use realia or visual aides (e.g., photographs, props, real objects), especially in science. A picture speaks a thousand words! Similarly, when possible I take them to the backyard to observe specific insects or plants, or even ask them to bring artifacts from home. When the topic does not lend to a simple observation, I resort to video clips, podcasts, or the video library in the school. We write down what they observe and then help them link this to their reading. The trick is to keep the reading and the observation really close in time and content to each other." (Melissa, fifth-grade science teacher)

3. **Dual-language instruction.** Maria, an ESL and reading teacher, helps students link knowledge across their two languages before they are encouraged to read the text in English. She acknowledges this is feasible for her because she is a native speaker of Spanish and because the majority of the ELs she works with speak Spanish at home. Having books on the same topics in both languages has facilitated this approach.

4. **Anticipation guides.** It can be beneficial to take a bit of extra time and have students go through an anticipation guide before reading the actual text (see example that follows). Cindy, a fourth-grade reading and science teacher, expressed that "the anticipation guide goes back and forth between what they anticipated or knew before they read and what they actually read. The going back and forth works when the guide does not interrupt their reading. I see it as a modified version of the KWL chart without the 'what-I-want-to-know' part."

A Word of Caution about Anticipation Guides

Anticipation guides are a great tool when you first introduce ABK or when you need a strong scaffold for students who really struggle with thinking of what they know about a topic before reading. However, anticipation guides are not replicable for independent reading, nor do they help with ABK throughout the reading of a text. For example, in Figure 3–5, the anticipation guide provides some general orientation to the topic of elephants and can help students to broadly activate

Leo and Lucas observe bees to activate prior knowledge before reading about bees.

Figure 3–5. Anticipation Guide for Expository Text. *Elephants* (2000) by Barbara Taylor. Southwater.

ANTICIPATION GUIDE

Name: Jane   Date: December 16

Title: Elephants   Author: Barbara Taylor

Statement.	Agree/ Disagree.	Were you right?	Reflect.
1. All elephants have tusks.	Agree	No	Female elephants in Asia don't have tusks. I wonder why.
2. Elephants can sleep standing up.	Agree	Yes	They probably have a hard time getting up after they lay down.
3. Elephants are the tallest land animal.	Disagree	Yes	I remembered that giraffes are taller.
4. Elephants only use their trunks for smelling.	Disagree	Yes	I've seen elephants on TV use their trunks to pick things up.
5. Elephants are herbivores (plant-eaters).	Disagree	No	I thought they ate bugs too.
6.			
7.			

Teacher: "Before we read the book *Elephants*, I want you to think about what you already know. Read this list of true and false statements. Make a prediction about each statement by deciding if you agree or disagree with it. Then record your answers in the second column. After we read the book, you can go back and see if your answers were correct."

Teacher: "Now that you have read the book, go back through the statements and your answers to determine whether or not you were correct. Then reflect on what you think about the predictions you made. Let's do the first one together: *All elephants have tusks*. I thought this statement was true before I read the book, so I wrote 'Agree,' but now I disagree. The book said female elephants in Asia do not have tusks. That's strange! I wonder why? I'm going to record these thoughts under the column that says, 'Reflect.'"

knowledge on the topic. However, if and when the text becomes more specific, the guide may fall short—it cannot cover the depth and breadth of a book. More importantly, if students get too used to anticipation guides, the scaffold they provide may be difficult to withdraw! So use them sparsely and, especially, early on when teaching ABK with students who seem to "go blank" when you encourage them to share their ABK.

Activating Background Knowledge *Throughout* Reading

Because the role of ABK is to enhance comprehension, students need to link their knowledge to specific sections in text; thus ABK should be implemented and taught not only before reading but *throughout* the reading of a text as well. Perhaps the emphasis on browsing the book and looking for text features made you think that ABK occurs at one point in time, and that this occurs before the actual reading of a text. It does not. The goal is for students to ABK independently and automatically, in ways that allow them to think of what they know before they approach new paragraphs or sections in text, and then they must link this knowledge to what they are reading. These text connections demonstrate that students are building integrated knowledge representations from the text, not just isolated pieces of knowledge. Similarly, another key indicator of effective background knowledge activation is the ability to integrate information across texts. Teachers may find that some ELs need to read different resources before reading a shared text so that they can share background knowledge with their classmates.

Over the years, both in my research and in my own classroom, I have seen the ways these background activation strategies can help ELs. For example, in a fifth-grade science classroom I visited, I observed a teacher using text features to help students activate what they knew about the solar system. The teacher's intention was for this strategy to improve focus on the text content while also bringing students' background experiences to it. When Emanuel, a student in this class, was asked how text features helped him with reading, he candidly stated: "I'm Hispanic and some words I don't understand, so reading opens a door to a whole 'nother world of words that I can learn. When I learned to use these features I saw the words that will help me think, what is it that I know about this book? My favorite ones are the pictures and the captions because they helped me really focus on learning about the solar system and our Earth." Emanuel shows that he knows how to make this strategy, activating background knowledge using text features, work for him. His choice of the word *favorite* argues for its effectiveness. When students choose *when* to use strategies and *which* strategies work best for them, we know we have achieved success. Furthermore, think again about Melissa, the fifth grader in Vanessa Shann's classroom (at the beginning of this chapter). She could clearly and precisely describe her areas of strength and needs-improvement after Vanessa's support for reading self-efficacy. Her experience relates to Emanuel's statement here—with step-by-step instruction on ABK, Emanuel can precisely describe the process he used to ABK and, possibly, he can also clearly identify this process as part of his reading. Remember that when we provide explicit, systematic comprehension strategy instruction and useful contingent feedback, we are contributing to our students' self-efficacy for reading. I encourage you to revisit the ideas in Figure 1.3, in Chapter 1, where I used our own and others' research to support instructional practices to promote self-efficacy for the whole act of reading—not just for one specific comprehension strategy. As you re-read these practices, though, consider how they can be fused with the instruction of ABK shared in this chapter. Then, you may want to consider how they can be merged with other comprehension strategies and techniques. Instruction that is carefully thought out to support self-efficacy leads to more competent learners and readers. Self-efficacy, in turn, becomes a crucial component of becoming an engaged reader.

Vocabulary Learning and Knowledge Goals

Developing the Language of Experts

With so many ideas about appropriate vocabulary instruction, especially for ELs, it's no wonder teachers need to boil them down to essential principles. In a workshop I conducted, fifth-grade teacher Tanya expressed her ideals for this area perfectly:

> *"Vocabulary instruction needs to be something that goes beyond us. Students need to be able to figure out words by themselves while reading, one way or the other. They need the tools that will make them independent language learners. How do we promote that? We start slowly but consistently. We show them how we go about figuring out new word meanings, we use research on word learning, and we try to develop word consciousness. Most important, we keep in mind that all students, ELs included, need to see the value of learning new words through reading—not just because they need new words for writing or for the test, but because new words mean new ideas!"*

Tanya's reflection echoes my belief too. We have to connect our EL students' words with the big ideas and concepts if we want them to be lifelong readers and learners. Effective vocabulary instruction has to happen within this framework. All students, and especially ELs, benefit from strong vocabulary instruction, which, in turn, increases their ability to comprehend what they read and lends to a feeling of satisfaction at being able to understand.

Given the strong connection between vocabulary and reading (Cunningham and Stanovich 1997), it is no surprise that the limited vocabulary of many ELs has been identified as a major source of their reading challenges (Burgoyne et al. 2010; Hutchinson et al. 2003). Literacy researchers have estimated that children must understand 98 percent of the words in text to gain adequate comprehension during the elementary school years (Carver 1994; Hu and Nation 2000). Therefore, even relatively small challenges in vocabulary knowledge could lead to large challenges in reading comprehension. And, as we know, problems in reading comprehension can have long-lasting effects on all types of learning in school.

Vocabulary Acquisition for ELs Takes Time

Acquiring the depth and breadth of knowledge of core concepts and ideas is not something that can or should be expected to happen right away. A recent national report confirms that ELs of Spanish-speaking households take an average of 4.2 years to develop the English proficiency necessary to reach a grade-specific score on an English language proficiency assessment (Greenberg 2015). But the same report states, "Addressing proficiency is more complicated than simply counting the number of years it takes a student to reach proficiency" (Greenberg 2015, 1).

Most ELs in U.S. classrooms, particularly those who are Spanish-speaking and come from low-income families, enter school with a more limited vocabulary in English than their English monolingual peers (Bialystok, Luk, and Kwan 2005; Mancilla-Martinez and Lesaux 2011; Umbel et al. 1992). Children's exposure to language in the home before they go to daycare, preschool, or elementary school forms the foundation of their language development, whichever language the parents speak comes more naturally to children. Researchers who looked at vocabulary differences among four-and-a-half-year-old Spanish-speaking ELs in three different types of homes—where mostly English is spoken, where mostly Spanish is spoken, and where both English and Spanish are spoken equally—found that children raised in English-speaking homes had significantly larger initial English vocabularies than the other two groups (Mancilla-Martinez and Lesaux 2011). This is not surprising; the more exposure children have to a specific language, the greater the likelihood they will develop that language (Gathercole 2002; Oller and Eilers 2002).

However, by the time these children were twelve years old, researchers found that the rate of English vocabulary growth of children in households where Spanish and English were spoken equally surpassed that of the mostly English group. This suggests that early Spanish use in ELs' homes does not interfere with the development of English vocabulary over time. In fact, researchers strongly recommend that to support EL's vocabulary knowledge and literacy development, parents should be encouraged to question, use dialogue, and do lots of storytelling from an early age in whatever style and language comes more naturally (e.g., Lesaux 2013; Snow, Porsche, Tabors, and Harris 2007). However, the same study also shows us that even though children in all three groups received their school instruction in English, their vocabulary was below average and the gap with national norms persisted (Mancilla-Martinez and Lesaux 2011). This is one more piece of evidence that tells us that we need to ensure that vocabulary instruction for ELs is not only within a framework of knowledge goals but that is overtly explicit.

Promoting a Mindset for Growth: Knowledge Goals

Our goal in vocabulary instruction is not to overwhelm our ELs with long lists of words they must learn right away. Instead, we want to focus on building a foundation of knowledge. To do this, we carefully select specific words that support that content learning along with explicit vocabulary strategy instruction and multiple opportunities to hear and use the words in a variety of contexts. Over time, this strategy is what enables children to read and understand the range of texts they will encounter in school (Lesaux 2013): "In the end, it is *depth* of knowledge about the world that is a difference maker in reading achievement" (Lesaux 2013). Learning new words should be driven by this purpose: Learning about key concepts within a domain or topic.

In Susan's and Katrina's third- and fourth-grade classrooms, students focused on concepts of ecology such as *reproduction, respiration, migration,* and *defense* in the life sciences. These concepts guided students' reading of informational texts on various animal types. Animal types varied within groups in a classroom, but the key concepts were shared. Expertise on specific animals was developed by different students, but all students deepened their knowledge and vocabulary about ecological concepts (Guthrie et al. 2004). This type of focus on knowledge goals for reading means organizing reading activities and purposes around core concepts that explain substantial principles of a domain or a content area (Cox and Guthrie 2002).

The idea of knowledge or learning goals for reading informational texts was first fully developed during the Concept-Oriented Reading Instruction (CORI) program in the mid-1990s and early 2000s (e.g., Guthrie and Wigfield 2000). However, researchers had by then documented that when students have knowledge, learning, or mastery goals—all of which are closely related—they see their abilities or skills as opportunities for improvement in relation to previous performance rather than a measure of how they compare to others (Alderman 2008). When students have knowledge goals organized around a conceptual theme—that is, when content is organized around "a limited set of powerful ideas (basic understandings and principles)" (Brophy 1999, 80)—they are motivated to increase their competence and succeed through their own effort. If we move this idea to vocabulary learning, we can see that organizing vocabulary instruction around key concepts within a domain may facilitate learning the core structure or basic understanding of a topic. In the example of fourth graders learning ecological concepts, we can think about how our ELs can learn essential words related to these key concepts and organize their learning around them. For example, a semantic map (i.e., related words) for the concept of *respiration* can include *breathing, oxygen, carbon dioxide, lungs, circulatory system, respiratory system, survival, pollution*, and so forth. As we discuss later in this chapter, word choices for instruction will also depend on the texts to be used as well as how crucial these are for ELs' current and future learning.

When a knowledge goal is the driving question of instruction, students engage in deep processing of text and comprehend more than when trivial facts or performance goals are emphasized (Benware and Deci 1984; Meece, Blumenfeld, and Hoyle 1988; Taylor, Pearson, Clark, and Walpole 2000). Also, knowledge goals " . . . provide motivation for students because they give a purpose for using different reading comprehension strategies. By having knowledge goals, students learn to use the strategies with greater effort, attention, and interest than in a context devoid of deep, conceptual themes" (Wigfield, Mason-Singh, Ho, and Guthrie 2014, 44). Seventh-grader Marina captured the role of knowledge goals in her learning nicely:

> "When I know where I am going with my learning I feel better. Knowing we would learn about the causes of the Great Depression next week helped me see why words such as *depression, stock market crash, corporation, drought, the dust bowl, strikes*, and *bread lines* are so important to my learning of this topic. It was like having a road map for my learning."

The other advantage to having knowledge goals for comprehension strategy instruction is that it extends the complexity of EL students' vocabulary. That is, by having key concepts articulated within a unit to learn from, vocabulary words within the unit can be better prioritized. Not every word unknown to ELs needs to be explicitly taught, but words that are key to reading comprehension and to the essential concepts or ideas with a unit should be. The three-tiered system developed by Beck and colleagues can be applied.

In terms used by Beck, McKeown, and Kucan (2013), *basic words,* words used in everyday conversation, are considered Tier 1 words; these are generally learned in the early grades. *General academic words,* such as *relative, vary, formulate,* and *accumulate,* are considered Tier 2 words and are far more likely to appear in written texts than in speech. They require explicit teaching most of the time for ELs. *Domain-specific words* could be considered Tier 3 words and are specific to a domain of study such as *lava, legislature, circumference,* and *aorta.* Like Tier 2 words, they need to be taught to ELs (and non-ELs alike!), but they need in-depth learning because they are generally the labels used for the key concepts within a domain, unit, or theme of study.

A good way to foster vocabulary learning with a knowledge-goals approach is to engage students in learning words that help unlock the meaning of the key concepts they are learning. For example, when learning is organized within a conceptual theme and the focus is on learning concepts, students have more options about how and what to read to satisfy their curiosity (Guthrie, Wigfield, and Perencevich 2004), while also promoting depth of processing and multiple encounters with words (Stahl and Fairbanks 1986). For example, a potential conceptual theme for grade 4 is "the hidden worlds of the wetlands." This theme was developed as part of our research on the CORI project to fit a unit within the grade 4 life science curriculum.

Sarah Bianco, a grade 4 science teacher of a self-contained EL class, and I developed a similar conceptual theme (Taboada, Bowerman, and Bianco 2012). Sarah focused on specific words such as *growth, nourishment, predator, prey, inhalation, exhalation,* and *carbon dioxide.* These are all words that needed to be unpacked to understand the key concepts. Sarah ensured that her students, who varied in their English proficiency quite a bit, had (a) opportunities for wide reading on key concepts, (b) ample definitional and contextual information for each concept, (c) multiple encounters with these words (e.g., Graves 2000; Stahl and Fairbanks 1986), and (d) opportunities to see how and why different concepts were related to each other.

In Sarah's classroom, students learned new words that were directly related to key concepts. When she communicated to students, they understood the idea that they were learning these words because of their association with the central concepts of the unit and their usefulness for specific knowledge of the subject matter (Tier 3 words) as well as for their use across subjects (Tier 2 words), rather than because they were on a vocabulary list that was disconnected from the rest of their learning and to be studied only for the sake of checking off an assignment or getting a grade. She had a list of words associated with each of the key concepts posted on the wall. When ELs are aware of this cognitive task—that they are expanding their conceptual frameworks along with their vocabulary—they can recognize how each small success creates something larger.

How to Support ELs' Vocabulary Development: A Model of Instruction

As many of you may have experienced in your own classroom, planning vocabulary instruction within the context of knowledge and content goals can be a challenge. It is hard to decide exactly how to develop vocabulary within a unit that supports all students and ELs in particular. The research is out there, but it often does not get to the classroom teachers who need it. In the discussion that follows, I outline four principles for vocabulary instruction that are well grounded in the latest research and that can be clearly applied in your classroom: (1) use engaging informational texts, (2) select a small set of essential academic words, (3) provide explicit instruction using multiple modalities (listening, speaking, reading, and writing), and (4) teach independent word-learning strategies.

Use Engaging Informational Texts in Instruction

As we noted in Sarah's life science unit, vocabulary instruction within the framework of conceptual themes provides a natural context for words that are, at the very least, semantically related. Thematically related words are neither random nor isolated but are chosen because of their association with central concepts and students' specific knowledge of the subject matter (Tier 3; domain-specific vocabulary) and for their utility across subject areas (Tier 2; general academic words).

Consider the following primary text for a unit in a sixth-grade class:

"Jefferson's message was secret because France owned the territory in question and such an expedition would surely be considered trespassing."

"The government was shrewd enough to realize that by mandating that the land could not lay idle they could easily avoid one problem and immediately solve another."

"Today is not so different from 1888 in that land remains one commodity that can't be created by mass production or any other method."

Clearly, the vocabulary used here is not that of daily conversation. The text includes Tier 2 and Tier 3 words. In reviewing this text the teacher might decide that general academic—Tier 2—words such as *considered, avoid, remains,* and *realize* will need explicit teaching or, at least, attention within the text. Furthermore, concepts central to the text, and possibly the unit/theme, are represented by domain-specific—Tier 3—words such as *expedition, trespassing, mandating,* and *commodity,* all of which are highly abstract and can make reading "between the lines" challenging for almost anybody. Such words, used in crucial places in the text, can result in misunderstandings even for native speakers of English. Obviously, the burden is even greater for ELs (e.g., Brown 2007).

So what would be some advantages of having several interesting, content-rich informational texts on westward expansion to use with this text? Along with the motivation to read widely and in-depth on a topic, and develop knowledge expertise as discussed earlier, we would also be developing ELs' background knowledge on the topic and reinforcing key concepts within the theme or unit across texts. ELs who are not familiar with westward expansion prior to reading the previous text will have a hard time making sense of the central ideas in it. Terms and concepts such as *exodusters, boomers, sooners,* and *immigrants* will likely be lost to them without proper introductions. Even simpler terms such as *flatlands, treeless wasteland, low rainfall,* and *land erosion*—all key to the western climate and with consequences for the new settlers—may be lost for ELs unless a variety of leveled texts are used to introduce them.

If we choose texts selectively around a theme—texts that are brief early on in the unit, engaging by force of the illustrations, vocabulary-rich and explicit (i.e., demonstrate good use of text features and have glossaries for vocabulary words), and interconnected within a unit of study—we make EL's academic vocabulary learning much smoother. Within our unit on westward expansion for Grade 7, we used a variety of trade books on several key topics that took into account (a) key concepts/ideas identified by social studies teachers and the state curricula, and (b) at least three reading levels (below, at, and above grade level) to cater to the English proficiency of ELs. Figure 4–1 includes a list of these texts as well as short videos that were used for concept and vocabulary development. Figure 4-2 provides recommendations for choosing informational texts.

Select a Small Set of Essential Academic Words

Vocabulary researchers strongly recommend selecting a small set of words for intensive, repeated, and in-depth use over the course of several lessons (Beck, McKeown, and Kucan 2002: Lesaux et al. 2010). A "small set" of words includes five to eight words from some selected texts to teach over the course of several lessons or a unit (see Figure 4-3). The exact number of words will depend on the age and grade of your students, the length and types of texts you select, and the

Figure 4–1. Examples of Leveled Texts and Video Clips for a Grade 7 Westward Expansion Unit

- *A Changing Nation: Immigration and Industrialization from the Civil War to World War I* by M. Burgan (whole-class reading)
- *You Wouldn't Want to Work on the Railroad! A Track You'd Rather Not Go Down* by I. Graham (small-group reading)
- *African-Americans in the Old West* by T. McGowen (small-group reading)
- *The Homestead Act* by E. Landau (small-group reading)
- Link to "American History: At the Western Frontier" from United Streaming: http://player .discoveryeducation.com/index.cfm?guidAssetID=C8A6DB97-1E49-43CA-9FDD -D146FD52B7DA&productcode=US
- Link to "Boom or Bust: Mining and the Opening of the American West" from United Streaming: http://player.discoveryeducation.com/index.cfm?guidAssetID=B544C7D0-5402-4432-8722 -04427466A801&productcode=US
- Link to PBS's Frontier House "Homestead History" essay: www.pbs.org/wnet/frontierhouse /frontierlife/essay1.html
- Link to "The Real American Cowboy" from United Streaming: http://player.discoveryeducation.com /index.cfm?guidAssetID=CEC1158B-127C-40C9-A01D-0C6670D983CA&productcode=US

Figure 4–2. Recommendations for Choosing Engaging Informational Texts that Support Academic Vocabulary Instruction*

- Early within a unit or theme texts should be brief and aimed to develop background knowledge on key, essential domain-specific concepts within the theme.
- Later in the unit or theme texts can be longer and focused on subtopics that contain target academic words around these subtopics (e.g., the Louisiana Purchase within westward expansion; closed circuits within a unit on electricity).
- The texts should be at different levels of difficulty within a topic to cater to different readers.
- Throughout the unit, the texts should connect to the unit /theme of study and help students build knowledge on the topic.
- They should spark immediate interest so that students want to read more about the topic.
- They should provide enough detail, text features, and examples so that students can increasingly comprehend on their own.
- The texts should contain ideas and key concepts that can be discussed from a variety of perspectives.

*Adapted from Baker et al. 2014; Guthrie, Wigfield, and Perencevich 2004.

amount of time devoted to each text within a unit (Baker et al. 2014). What criteria should we use for choosing these words that have rich potential for learning in-depth and across texts? The following criteria (adapted from Baker et al. 2014) has been determined to help teachers choose words for ELs; take note, however, that not all of the criteria needs to apply to each word you choose for instruction.

Figure 4–3. Small Sets of Essential Academic Words (repeated words are in italics)

Unit 1: Players with Pride	Unit 2: High-Tech Bullies	Unit 3: New Clues to a Mystery	Unit 4: Separated at School
affect culture community contribute establish ethnic/ethnicity residents welfare	communicate identity/identify incidents legally method policy research require survey	ancient area complex integrated located major period puzzle *researcher* site which	*community* discrimination distinctions evidence gender options regulations research respond since *survey* topic
Unit 5: Bad News for Bees	Unit 6: Do Kids Tune in Too Much?	Unit 7: Witness to History	Unit 8: Going the Distance
aware collapse conduct *contribute* crucial *identify* *research* resource seeking theory transport widespread yet	according average expert foundation media nearly percent (%) *survey*	*area* *awareness/aware* civil documentary image inspire issue *research* social survive vision while	anticipate constantly *contribute* convince effect expanse generate *inspire* *image* *researcher* releasing region *survive* until

Source: Lesaux et al. (2010).

- **Choose words that are essential.** Choose texts that have central concepts or facts to build knowledge on the key concepts within a unit or a theme (see Figure 4–3 for some examples of different units for a middle school curriculum (Lesaux et al. 2010). Then, preselect words that are linked to those concepts within a given text. Today publishers tend to bold those "key words"; however, attend to the bold as well as to the not-bold words that are key to understanding the text and the key concepts at hand.
- **Choose words that are frequently used and have multiple meanings.** Choose Tier 2 general academic words that are repeatedly used across texts and that students may encounter across content areas. These words

generally have multiple meanings; for example, *volume* refers to a book or series in ELA, but refers to the amount of space a body occupies in math and geometry. Beck, McKeown, and Kucan (2013) suggest that a word falls within the Tier 2 category if students already have ways to express the concept that the word represents and if they are able to explain the meaning of the word using words they already know. Figure 4–4 shows a selection of Tier 2 words and definitions that students are likely to be able to provide.

- **Choose words that are semantically and morphologically related** (Graves 2000, 2006; Lesaux et al. 2010). As you choose your words, present a small number of words that are related in meaning and have similar word parts. Specifically, words with affixes (prefixes and/or suffixes) allow attention to how word parts change a word's meaning or grammatical/ morphological form. For example, adding the prefix *un-* to the word *inspiring* changes the word's meaning, whereas adding the suffix *-ed* to *generate* changes it from present to past. I discuss morphological awareness in more detail later in this chapter.

Provide Explicit Instruction Using Multiple Modalities (Listening, Speaking, Reading, Writing)

In addition to explicit instruction of words and word-learning strategies, students need to learn vocabulary in authentic contexts, through a variety of modalities and by reading material in which the target words get meaning from, and support the meaning of, other words in the text (Nagy and Townsend 2012). This is true for all words, but for late elementary and middle school students it is especially true for academic vocabulary, both cross-discipline, general words (Tier 2), and discipline-specific words (Tier 3). For example, the words *polynomial, cytoplasm,* and *federalism* are unique to math, science, and social studies respectively (Nagy and Townsend 2012). Because discipline-specific words represent key concepts within a particular domain, students need *repeated exposure to these words in context* and through various modalities such as speaking, writing, and listening.

There are many ways to implement this idea. For example,

Figure 4–4. Tier 2 Words

Tier 2 Words	Students' Likely Expressions
merchant	salesperson or clerk
comment	something someone has to say
tend	take care of
maintain	keep going
emerging	coming out
fortunate	lucky
benevolent	kind

to foster vocabulary learning in science, Silverman and Hines (2009) led teachers to combine read-alouds with videos on biomes, such as the rainforest and the savannah in kindergarten through grade 2. They found that combining the videos with the read-alouds was particularly helpful for vocabulary learning of ELs in kindergarten through grade 2. Video-enhanced vocabulary that includes listening to explanations and viewing these concepts graphically benefited these students even more than it benefited their English-speaking peers (Silverman and Hines 2009). Similarly, grade 7 teachers used video clips to introduce key concepts in social studies units (e.g., portions of *Gone with The Wind* to introduce the Civil War) and generate discussion before or after reading as a way to build background knowledge. They found that learning key concepts through the video clips improved ELs' background knowledge, and particularly helpful for ELs' vocabulary learning was video accompanied by explicit instruction on comprehension strategies and graphic organizers built by students (Vaughn et al. 2009).

Teach Independent Word-Learning Strategies

Regardless of how carefully words are chosen for instruction, explicitly teaching words alone is not sufficient to build an adequate vocabulary. The focus on specific words must be accompanied by instruction in word-learning strategies that sets students up to figure out word meanings on their own.

Context Clues

There are two types of contexts: instructional and naturally occurring. The former provides helpful context for determining word meaning; the latter, less so. Authors of instructional texts intentionally craft the text so that key words are relatively easily figured out (Beck et al. 2013). Here is an example:

> The two cultures differed in other ways as well. They spoke different languages. They also had different **values**, or things that were important to them. Their differences made it hard for them to understand each other. (Rossi 2002, 7)

In this excerpt, the author identifies the potentially difficult word in bold type and includes an *appositive,* a noun or noun phrase that renames the word. (Here, I've done the same thing, although the defined word is in italics.) However, even in instructional texts many words necessary for understanding ideas go undefined.

Texts not specifically designed for instruction rarely provide this type of support. For example, in *Julie of the Wolves* (1972), Jean Craighead George writes, "Miyax stared hard at the regal black wolf, hoping to catch his eye. She must somehow tell him that she was starving and ask him for food" (6). From this context, a student might determine that the word *regal* implies generous, alert, curious, or any number of other attributes. The purpose of naturally occurring texts is to tell a story or describe a situation, not convey the meaning of a set of words or a particular concept. Most fiction authors choose the most fitting words to illustrate their idea without stopping to define them (Stahl and Nagy 2006). This is true in informational texts sometimes as well. It is, therefore, difficult for students to determine the meanings of many words in naturally occurring, non-instructional contexts.

How do we teach how to use context clues? Given that the use of context clues can lead and promote independence from the learner for vocabulary learning, it is a good idea to teach students to use context clues by following the guided release of responsibility model (See Figure 4–5). This involves teachers first modeling the instructional sequence and gradually releasing responsibility for using this sequence to students so they can use it on their own (Beck, McKeown, and Kucan 2013). Vocabulary researchers have suggested the following instructional sequence to help students use context clues: (1) generate hypotheses about what a word might mean, (2) evaluate those hypotheses, and (3) decide when to use a second strategy (e.g., using word parts or resources) to determine the word's exact meaning (Beck et al. 2013; Goerss, Beck, and McKeown 1999; Stahl and Nagy 2006).

Teaching these steps or using them as a fixed set or a checklist is not the intention. Rather, they should be used by teachers to model students' thinking about how to use context clues and determine the meanings of unknown words. Most important, students need to realize that they should generate and revise their hypotheses, and these hypotheses should not just be shot-in-the-dark guesses, but be supported by clues in the text and by their knowledge of word parts or morphological awareness (i.e., roots, prefixes, and suffixes).

Morphological Awareness

Morphological awareness is defined as "identifying the prefixes, suffixes, bases, and Greek and Latin roots and understanding *how* they combine to form words" (Templeton 2012, 117). *Morphology* is the branch of linguistics that comprises word structure and the way words are formed from *morphemes,* the smallest units of meaning. The ability to reflect on, analyze, and manipulate morphemes, or parts of words—that is, knowing that adding the suffix *-er* to *teach* will change the grammatical category from verb to noun, or that adding the suffix *-ed* can change a verb from present to past tense—is the essence of morphological awareness.

Figure 4–5. Learning to Use Context Clues

- **Read or reread the passage, and then discuss the overall meaning of the passage.** The goal here is to provide some context for the unknown words and not to zoom in on them directly without having a broader sense of the text surrounding the unknown word.
- **Posit an initial hypothesis about what the unknown word might mean, along with a justification for that hypothesis.** For example, Sarah, the fourth-grade science teacher portrayed earlier, shows her students how she hypothesizes the meaning of the term *monotony* in a text about the frozen ground of the Arctic Tundra.

  "Hmmm. I'm not sure what the word *monotony* means here. Let's see if I can figure out its meaning by coming up with my hypothesis, or my idea to try to explain what it means. One way to do this is to pretend that the unknown word is just a blank in the sentence. For example, 'Not a tree grew anywhere to break the _____ of the gold-green plain, for the soils of the tundra are permanently frozen.' Let's think about this sentence and if the word *monotony* fits in it. I know we talked about tundra when we first started reading this book, and it means a flat, treeless region where the ground is frozen. This sentence says that again. Maybe *monotony* means the 'frozen ground.'"

  Often, teachers hypothesize the correct meaning of the word because they already know it and think this is a good way to teach it to students, instead of, for instance, considering which clues students are likely to hone in on. Imagining and modeling a blank where the word can be placed is helpful to focus students on the clues that may or may not exist in the context surrounding the word.

- **Test your hypothesis to see if it makes sense by rereading the text and inserting your hypothesized meaning. Read around the word (either by rereading the sentences leading up to the word or by reading on).**

  "Let me see if that makes sense, 'Not a tree grew anywhere to break the monotony of the green-gold plain, for the soils of the tundra are permanently frozen.' It could be that, it seems to make sense: 'Breaking the gold-green plain' means breaking something that is similar, that does not change. Perhaps here it refers to the frozen ground without trees . . . it is all the same landscape, no trees, no variation."

  Encourage students to check how their hypothesized meaning fits by reading beyond the target sentence:

  "Does that fit? 'Not a tree grew anywhere to break the lack of variety of the gold-green plain, for the soils of the tundra are permanently frozen. Only moss, grass, lichens, and a few hardy flowers take root in the thin upper layer that thaws briefly in summer.' Yeah! After reading that follow-up sentence, that makes so much sense."

- **For verification, encourage students to try another strategy, such as using word parts and generating additional hypotheses.** Students are often happy to have come up with one possible answer, but it is important to use different word-learning strategies to generate multiple hypotheses that they can test. Additionally, it is important for students to recognize when context clues are not able to give them sufficient information to determine a word's meaning. For example, one way Sarah used word parts (roots) to analyze the word *monotony* was:

  "To make sure I am on the right track I will break the word *monotony* apart. I know from class that *mono-* means one. Hmmm. The first thing that comes to mind when I think of the word part *mono-* in Spanish are *monopatín* and *monólogo*—the former meaning a scooter, which is 'one skate,' and the latter meaning a speech by one person (like *monologue* in English). And I am pretty sure that *-tony* comes from 'tone' or 'sound,' like in music class. So *monotony* is likely to mean 'one sound.'"

(continues)

Figure 4–5. Learning to Use Context Clues *(continued)*

Other strategies could include the use of vocabulary resources such as dictionaries or glossaries (see the upcoming discussion about using dictionaries). However, whenever possible, teach and encourage students to use word parts (see the "Morphological Awareness" section that follows). The use of word parts will save students time, at least in the long run, and potential confusion that may arise from complex dictionary definitions.

- **Lastly, summarize what the passage means given your new understanding of the word.** This part is important because it wraps up the conversation with a succinct sentence explaining what the passage meant in light of the new word. This can help students focus on the meaning so they can comprehend the remainder of the passage.

    "It must have just looked plain and green-gold without any trees or really any plants; everything just looked the same and boring. That is what *monotony*, or something being *monotonous*, means in this context."

There are four main research-based instructional approaches to teaching students about and training them in morphological awareness (Carlisle et al. 2010), although, as always, this instruction should be folded into a comprehensive program of literacy instruction rather than taught in isolation.

1. *Heighten students' awareness of the morphological structure.*
   Breaking apart words and finding common morphemes in words are starting points in morphological awareness (Carlisle 2010). One way to foster students' awareness of word parts is to model noticing word parts when you come across an unknown word during a read-aloud. Another way to help students do this is through word sorts. For example, choose two or three word parts to focus on, generate lists of words that contain those parts, shuffle the words, and require students to sort the words based on their root or word part similarities. Figure 4–6 shows how words that have a prefix meaning "not" have been sorted according to the spelling of that prefix.

2. *Explicitly teach the meanings of affixes and base words.*
   As you heighten students' awareness of word parts, also teach them the meanings of specific prefixes, suffixes, and word roots/base words. Generally, first teach common prefixes, then common suffixes, and then common word roots—all depending on your students' levels of morphological awareness. Word parts can be posted on a word wall dedicated solely to affixes and word roots, or word parts in whole words can be distinguished in some way. Spelling lists can also emphasize word parts; morphological awareness and spelling are connected (Carlisle 2010).

3. *Foster morphological problem solving* (Anglin 1993).
   Once students are aware of word parts and know the meaning of some of those parts, teach them to use this knowledge to determine the meanings of unknown words. Model thinking aloud about the constituent

parts of words and what they might mean. For example, when introducing a unit on geometry, you might notice that *geo-* means "earth," *-metr* means "measure," and *-y* is a suffix that indicates "characterized by." Put together, these parts suggest that *geometry* is characterized by measuring the Earth. Then look at the context to see whether this hypothesis fits. In this way, you are combining students' understanding of context clues and word parts with problem solving about words.

One can also create matrices that show how a root word can be combined with various prefixes and suffixes to make new words. Word matrices, introduced gradually (starting with very few words and roots), are excellent ways to help ELs see the similarities of word roots in English and their first language. For example, in the matrix in Figure 4–7, the box in the center is the word root or base (in this case, *dict*). The boxes on the left contain prefixes and on the right suffixes. One can use the word *matrix* to make many different words, like *contradict* or *contradictory* or *dictate* or *dictator*. When students learn how to use the matrices, they quickly learn many words at one time, and the morphology or roots of words. One can teach them how the meaning of *dict* helps them to understand *contradict* and *dictator*. One can also make them notice the *Spanish friend* (a word that shares the same Latin root with English) (Beck, McKeown, and Kucan 2013) at the bottom of Figure 4–7. The word *decir* in Spanish comes from the same Latin root as *dict*. This link, www.realspellers.org/resources/matrices, has a variety of teacher-created matrices that can be helpful when thinking about word morphology and derivations.

Figure 4–6. Word Sort Based on the Roots *im-* and *in-*

im-	in-
immature	incorrect
imperfect	inedible
impractical	inappropriate
impossible	infamous
impolite	informal

4. *Apply morphological problem solving to unknown words encountered in reading.*
   This approach truly helps students become independent word learners. Students can learn to analyze word parts in isolation with relative ease, but applying this strategy to new words encountered in text may prove more difficult. As you teach your students about word parts, also teach them to notice, build, and deconstruct words as part of their reading while also maintaining the meaning of the text.

Figure 4–7. Word Matrix

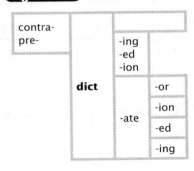

Spanish friend: decir, to speak

Academic Vocabulary Instruction for ELs: An Example from Research

Researchers combined all of these principles—teaching semantically and morphologically related words, teaching word-learning strategies, reading widely—to develop effective vocabulary instruction for middle school ELs (Lesaux et al. 2010) by putting together an eight-day lesson cycle for each of eight two-week units. Each unit was anchored by an article from *Time for Kids* magazine that was selected on the basis of readability level, appealing topic (for example, single-gender classrooms, television viewing rates, diversity issues), length, and opportunities for teaching academic vocabulary. Nine or ten academic words semantically related to the unit and morphologically related to each other were selected for each unit (see Figure 4–3). The Weekly Lesson Plan that follows offers those first five lessons in detail as designed by Lesaux and colleagues (2010). This particular unit is anchored by the "Separated at School" article about single-gendered schools. During this week, students move from understanding the concept of an issue, to building a vocabulary around it, and then finally applying those words in different contexts. Preselected words for this unit included *discrimination, distinctions, evidence, gender, options, regulations research, respond, since, survey,* and *topic.* In addition, you will see the findings from the latest research that supports the instructional choices described. Finally, Figure 4–8 shows the skills that could extend from this week with the target words introduced on Day One (Lesaux 2010).

Figure 4–8.   Week Two and Beyond

SKILL	PRACTICE	RESEARCH that Supports This Practice
Students use the target words outside of the context of the article.	Conduct mock interviews by creating questions with target words.	Scholars highlight that negotiating multiple meanings and multiple shades of meaning for a word is important to successful recognition and use of word meanings (e.g., Stahl and Nagy 2006).
In pairs, students prewrite by using graphic organizers to categorize their ideas. Students include target words in this process.	Create a debate question, "Would single-gendered middle schools make students more successful?" Then design a pro/con graphic organizer for students to complete.	Skilled writers are more knowledgeable about the process of writing than less skilled writers (e.g., Saddler and Graham 2007).
Students use target words in an independent piece of writing.	Using a graphic organizer, students write a paragraph on the topic of the unit.	Given the reciprocal relationship between reading and writing (e.g., Graves and Watts-Taffe 2002), authentic opportunities to use words in extended writing can serve as ways to consolidate knowledge of word meanings.

Adapted from Lesaux et al. (2010).

WEEKLY LESSON PLAN AT A GLANCE

Day One: Introduce an engaging informational text, "Separated at School."

- What's the Point?

Rather than simply memorizing vocabulary, students will be invested and engaged in learning concepts and acquiring background knowledge as they read the text and will begin to map labels (words) onto these new concepts. Using the text to introduce an engaging topic also provides a meaningful context for discussing the words throughout the unit. It is important to define the word as well as to relate it back to the context (sentence, paragraph) of the text. A range of studies have supported the importance of both definitional and contextual information (Stahl and Fairbanks 1986; Stahl and Nagy 2006).

- Activities to Build Vocabulary:

    1. Read article as a class and discuss the key concepts.
    2. Introduce target words explicitly—how to spell a target word; what a word looks like; what it sounds like; what I, my teacher, and classmates know about its meaning.

- HOW TO . . . ask questions your students will want to answer.

    - _What have teachers noticed in single-gender classrooms?_
    - _Do teachers believe this experiment is working?_
    - _Would you like this class to be a single-gender class?_

Day Two: Introduce a small set of vocabulary words with rich potential from the article/text.

- What's the Point?

With input and discussion about the words' meanings from the text, the teacher, and classmates, students will begin to form an accurate understanding of the words. The teacher will be able to build on students' prior knowledge while immediately clarifying any misinformation as the students share their ideas aloud. This is based on cognitive research that indicates the importance of schema activation before developing more intricate and complex schema (Bransford 2004); that is, starting with the meaning of the target words in the context of the article (a simpler schema), other word meanings can be discussed (a more complex word schema). Also, research recommends activating and building on students' word knowledge prior to introducing formal definitions, in order to refine vague understandings and correct misunderstanding (Marzano and Pickering 2005).

- Activities to Build Vocabulary:

  - Introduce how to use context clues as a word-learning strategy.
  - Brainstorm word meanings within and outside the meaning of the text.
  - Create class definitions using accurate information.
  - Create and record personal definitions by rephrasing class definition in students' own words.

- HOW TO . . . generate informal definitions.

  To generate informal definitions, students write down all they know about this word. After a few minutes, students share word knowledge. As a large group, the teacher confirms the definitions, posts accurate information, and contributes necessary additional information to define each word. Finally, the class comes up with informal definitions using information generated together.

Day Three: Answer text-based questions using target words as whole group and pairs.

- What's the Point?

  Students apply information drawn from dictionary and personal definitions as they work together to answer literal and inferential questions from the text. This allows them to use target words in a scaffolded, highly contextualized situation, first orally and then in writing. This idea is based on several research studies that emphasize the importance of deep processing through oral and written activities (Beck, McKeown, and Kucan 2002; Carlo et al. 2004; Graves 2006; Stahl and Nagy 2006).

- Activities to Build Vocabulary:

  - Answer text-based questions using target words as a whole group and in pairs.
  - Share answers with classmates orally.

■ HOW TO . . . scaffold think-pair and reader response.

Have the questions written on the board. Then, say to students:

"With a partner, discuss the following questions before writing your own answer in your notebook:

- *What evidence will the school officials use to decide whether the program is working and should be continued?*
- *How do students respond differently in single-gender classrooms?*
- *What kind of discrimination against girls happened regularly before Title IX?"*

You may have students talk about each question and then write. Or, for more English-proficient ELs, you may have a designated time to talk and then offer time to write. Encourage students to share as a large group. Scaffolding pair-thinking comes from research that highlights the importance of creating scenarios around words such that the use of the words in these scenarios fosters deep word processing (Beck, McKeown, and Kucan 2002; Carlo et al. 2004; Graves 2006; Stahl and Nagy 2006).

Day Four: Sketch a representation of the target word and write a related sentence.

■ What's the Point?

By making a visual representation of the target word and creating a sentence that uses the word accurately, students move toward a much deeper understanding of the word. Both of these tasks entail a metacognitive aspect allowing them to enhance their understanding of their own learning process. These tasks are based on research highlighting that depicting a word graphically, as in a picture, symbol, or a graphic organizer, they are encouraged to think of it in a totally different way (Marzano and Pickering 2005). Also, asking students to make judgments about the sensical or nonsensical use of words in sentences provides opportunities for deep processing (Carlo et al. 2004).

■ Activities to Build Vocabulary:

Sketch a representation of a target word (e.g., a crossword puzzle, or a sentence-judgment task such as determining whether a target makes sense within a sentence), and then write a related sentence.

▪ HOW TO . . . model a think-aloud to visualize vocabulary.

As you draw on a whiteboard or use a document camera focused on your piece of paper, you could think aloud while sketching the word *discrimination:*

I know that discrimination refers to when a person is treated unfairly for any number of reasons, such as age or gender or race or religion. This is a bit of a hard one to draw, but I think I am going to make a picture of a kids' clubhouse and I am going to put a sign on the door that says, "No girls allowed!" While this is just a kids' clubhouse, it is still discrimination.

After you model this example, take another word on the list, such as *options*. Engage students in the thinking by asking them what you should draw. Encourage them to give reasons for their ideas. Finally, ask students to do a third word independently or in pairs.

Day Five: Teach morphology as part of an independent word-learning strategy.

▪ What's the Point?

Teaching morphology, such as suffixes and prefixes directly, gives students an understanding of how words are related and how they can figure out unknown words by using word parts. This lesson addresses both word-specific knowledge (e.g., different forms of the target words) and word-general skills (e.g., how to be metacognitive about breaking down words). Many studies have shown the benefits of morphology instruction (Baumann et al. 2002; Carlo et al. 2004).

▪ Activities to Build Vocabulary:

- Teach specific target suffixes directly.
- Lead whole-class discussion to complete a word form chart using forms of the target words.
- Provide student practice with making and recognizing word forms in writing and revising activities related to the theme of the text.

▪ HOW TO . . . explicitly teach a suffix.

It is important to remember to take time to teach ELs the parts of words, including suffixes. In a lesson, here is how I might introduce the suffix *–al*.

–al *is like the other suffixes we've learned because it changes the part of speech of the word.* –al *changes words from nouns (person, place, thing, or idea) into adjectives (describes a word). So if there is a person who does magic, I could describe her by saying that she is* magical. *Magic is a thing or a noun, but* magical *is the way you would describe someone or something, so that makes* magical *an adjective.*

New Academic Vocabulary Research Brings New Understandings for Teachers

As you can tell from this chapter, there has been a proliferation of research on vocabulary instruction for both ELs and English-native speakers in the past two to three decades. There are many ways to teach words and several research principles that guide criteria on how to choose words for instruction. In addition, as a field, we know quite a bit about how to teach students to develop word-learning strategies so that they can become less teacher-dependent and more self-directed in their vocabulary learning. My recommendation is that you take the ideas and principles provided in this chapter as guidelines for instruction and then, when you decide to adopt a vocabulary program or vocabulary practices, you do so on the basis of having explored the research behind them. Vocabulary programs that are multifaceted in nature, as the one portrayed in this chapter developed by Lesaux and colleagues, use multiple techniques and instructional components to build word knowledge and word-learning strategies. Therefore, it is important for teachers to understand the principles and research behind each component. Although we are (hopefully) a long way from having students memorize vocabulary lists prior to a unit, much of the vocabulary teaching still observed in classrooms today is far from being research based, nor are these practices conducive to sound and lasting word knowledge. Thus, my emphasis is on understanding the practice as well as the research behind it.

In addition, I strongly believe that as important as word knowledge is for EL's language development, vocabulary learning should be done in the broader context of engaging comprehension strategy instruction. This instruction should be comprised of engaging texts, include motivation practices, and focus on comprehension in a holistic, broad way so that word learning is woven with strategy use whenever possible. Given space constraints, in this chapter I only focused on one motivation practice—the use of knowledge goals for instruction. However, many of the motivation supports included in other chapters can be fused with vocabulary instruction. Focusing on the key concepts underlying a topic of study and targeting key essential concepts by having knowledge goals guide instruction are good ways to organize criteria for selecting words to teach. In this way, vocabulary learning and instruction are subservient to the broader and more motivating goal of building knowledge, in depth and over time.

Teaching Resources

- Templeton, Bear, Invernizzi, and Johnston's (2010) book, *Vocabulary Their Way: Word Study with Middle and Secondary Students,* is a great resource for learning more about teaching vocabulary to students in the upper grades. It includes lists of prefixes, suffixes, and word roots that students should know, as well as templates for games and activities.
- *Words Their Way: Word Study for Phonics, Vocabulary, and Spelling Instruction* (Bear et al. 2012) provides a similarly great resource of prefixes, suffixes, and word roots that students should know. It also includes templates for games and activities.
- *No More "Look Up the List" Vocabulary Instruction (Not This But That)* by Charlene Cobb and Camille Blachowicz (authors), and Nell K. Duke and Ellin Oliver Keene (editors) (Heinemann 2014). Like other books in the *Not This But That* series, this one provides a great overview of why widely held practices, such as looking up words and writing sentences or completing worksheets, just do not work. Great ideas on what we can do instead are shared.
- http://ies.ed.gov/ncee/wwc/publications_reviews.aspx. This is the latest Institute of Education Sciences (IES) guide on recommendations for vocabulary instruction of ELs. You will see many of their ideas reflected in this chapter, but I strongly encourage you to take a look at it. It is full of practical ideas that are well supported by research!
- www.wordandphrase.info is a website created by Mark Davies, a professor of linguistics at Brigham Young University. He has created a new list of the most frequently occurring academic vocabulary words. *Word and Phrase* can help you identify which academic vocabulary words to teach your students and to analyze written work to determine the frequency of higher-level words.

- The Online Etymology Dictionary can be found at www.etymonline.com. This resource will tell you about the origin of words in English. Just be careful, as this website was designed for adults and includes even lascivious origins of words.
- *Word Stems: A Dictionary* (Kennedy 1996) is a great reference book to have on hand to quickly look up the meaning of a prefix, suffix, or word root.
- Word Searcher (www.neilramsden.co.uk/spelling/searcher/) is a website that allows you to search for a particular word part. When you enter the word part, it will generate a list of words that contain those letters in that order. Not all of the words generated will have the meaning of that word part. For example, if you search for *pre-*, one of the words generated will be *preach,* which does not meaningfully decompose into *pre-ach*. However, you will also find the word *precook,* which does meaningfully decompose into *pre-cook*. It is an interesting activity to have students examine the words that are generated and determine which are meaningful. Merriam-Webster's online dictionary for kids can be found at http://www.word central.com/. It also has a section titled "Build your own dictionary," which is a repository for words created and defined by students.

5

Determining Importance
Main Ideas and Topic Relevance

Learning to Focus on the Text

Determining what is important in life is no small thing. The events of one day can pull us in so many different directions that at the end of the day we're more aware of the pressure of the tugging than of attending to any one thing. This kind of skill set is the same kind of thinking we teach students when we teach the main idea. Although some people might contend that main ideas do not exist in the real world but only on standardized tests, identifying the main idea is an essential tool to help ensure that one is holding onto the meaning of the text itself. This is not a simple task, however. When we ask our students to consider how to determine importance, even within the constraints of one text, there are many aspects of the text to consider. The parameters of importance are defined by context, and all students, not just struggling readers or ELs, need to know the difference between what is important to them, *the reader*—because it is new or interesting information—versus what is important *to the author*—because he or she structured the text to communicate a hierarchy of ideas.

How the reader determines importance varies with types of text and genres, as well as with the readers' interest and background knowledge. For the reader, an interesting detail may be the most important idea in a text. However, for accuracy of comprehension the reader needs to be able to distinguish between what is most important to the reader and what is most important to the text. In reading an Earth science article, I'm surprised and amazed to learn that tardigrades, a micro-animal, can go dormant in adverse environmental conditions by drying out to three percent or less water and then rehydrate when conditions improve. Fascinating, no doubt, and I may choose to learn more about tardigrades after reading this article, but what is the article mainly about? It's about the possibility of life on Mars. In the ten-page article, two paragraphs explain that tardigrades are Earth creatures most likely to be able to live on Mars. Although my engagement with that detail proves that I comprehended that section of the article, it doesn't prove that I understood the article as a whole. Of course, our reading lives include this kind of free-range gathering of information. But, when the purpose of our reading is to learn about a specific topic and to improve our ability to read complex texts, we need to show that we have a clear sense of the text as a whole to explain how the details work collectively to communicate larger ideas. This is especially true for informational texts where the hierarchy of ideas is key to building knowledge. Certainly, asking a student what he finds interesting in a text is a good way to begin a conversation assessing that student's comprehension of the text, but then we need to assess whether the student's understanding goes beyond that detail and whether he can connect details to the larger ideas in the text. When our goal is to improve ELs' comprehension of content area texts, teaching informational text structures is one of the best uses of our instructional time. Students need exposure to different text structures, including compare and contrast, time lines, or hierarchical diagrams. We need to help them connect the structure with the comprehension of the content in informational texts, and make them aware there may be a single main idea or several.

In the digital age, when children are surrounded by a variety of text formats and can click back and forth between texts, separating the essential from the non-essential can be challenging (Keene and Zimmermann 2007; Harvey and Goudvis 2007). But this is not just a problem with digital texts. Ironically, it can be even more difficult to decide what is most important in a well-written text because the ideas are tightly compressed. The different formats and varying text structures of informational texts mean that ELs often struggle, highlighting or underlining whole paragraphs because they cannot decide which text sections are the most important and may not fully understand what differentiates a main idea from a supporting detail. Consider the following passage from *The Iroquois: People of the Northeast,* by R. Maile:

Deskaheh was born in 1872 on the Grand River Reservation [in Canada]. This was the reservation that Joseph Brant helped create. Deskaheh belonged to the Cayuga, one of the six Iroquois nations. After he finished high school, Deskaheh went to the United States and worked as a lumberjack in the Allegheny Mountains. Then he returned home to Grand River and took up farming. He married and had nine children. (24)

One main idea is that Deskaheh was an Iroquois. However, his having worked in the United States and then having farmed with his family back in Canada is also important. There is not just one main idea but two or three, depending on what we already know about Deskaheh and the Iroquois people, what resonates with our experiences, or what we feel the author is trying to emphasize. As a teacher, our job is to help students navigate through this type of text, guiding them to a clearer understanding. I'll provide some detail about how to do this later in the chapter.

ELs' Struggles with Identifying Main Ideas

Students, especially struggling EL readers, need to understand that some text sections (paragraphs first, longer passages later) have one main idea that is generally supported by details. If students can't track the development of an idea in the text, then they cannot monitor their comprehension and are more likely to have a hazy or incorrect understanding of the text. This, in turn, leads students to hold onto very little information from the text. Being able to identify the main idea in a text is not an isolated task of comprehension; rather, it connects to the larger foundation of academic knowledge that we expect children to gather as they travel through school. In short, if students cannot identify the main idea in a text, it is unlikely that they are building new knowledge over time.

Most students say they can identify the main idea in an informational text, but our research suggests otherwise. Out of 149 sixth graders in our USHER program (Taboada and Buehl 2011)—of whom 66 percent were Spanish-speaking ELs—64 percent reported understanding a passage they read well or very well, but only 9 percent correctly identified main ideas without confusing them with supporting details. Because ELs are learning word labels and their meaning simultaneously, teaching them to determine key ideas is twice as important, as it is easy for ELs to get derailed by words that are not essential to key understandings. In addition, if ELs are not explicitly taught to determine important ideas in a short paragraph, they may think everything is important. If everything is deemed important, then the likelihood to hold onto anything is significantly decreased! We understand texts by building relationships about importance through conceptual networks. For example, in the excerpt below we start forming a conceptual network by understanding which words explain (*hair, milk-producing glands*) and which words label categories (*mammal*), and the specific context where that network applies.

There are more than 4,000 species of mammals. Mammals have certain common features: They all have four legs, they have bodies covered by hair, a stable and high body temperature, they breathe through a muscle called the diaphragm and all females have milk-producing glands. (http://www.scienceclarified.com/loMa/Mammals.html)

When we give ELs a criterion for selecting a few key ideas that are more important than others, we show them how to build conceptual knowledge from text.

Many ELs have poor comprehension even if they have adequate decoding skills (Lesaux, and Geva 2006). Even when paragraphs are relatively short, struggling readers neglect to reread sentences with meaning that is unclear to them, and they get lost in the details. Much of this struggle comes from an absence of instruction on how to identify the main idea explicitly. In other words, struggling readers often receive an overemphasis on instruction at the word level at the expense of learning explicit comprehension strategies and genre characteristics (Riches and Genessee 2006). Strategy instruction isn't the only component of comprehension instruction, but it is a particularly effective one (e.g., Vaughn et al. 2009), especially for ELs who respond well to teaching that explicitly shows them how to apply strategies flexibly to accessible text at their level (Taboada et al. 2015; Taboada, Bianco, and Bowerman 2012; Vaughn et al. 2009).

This research is supported by our classroom data as well. After receiving explicit instruction on main ideas for three weeks, 30 percent of grades 6 and 7 ELs—versus only 9 percent before instruction—were able to correctly identify main ideas and distinguish them from other nonrelevant details (Taboada Barber and Ramirez, under review). Tomas said, **"It has helped me find the most important things and organize them in my head; it broke it down for me to understand it better."** Abril told us, **"I can understand better when I find main ideas and details because I stop reading casually when I am looking for them. When I read casually I get confused, especially with history books."** Attending to important information over several sentences, organizing information, breaking down text into its components, and reading with a specific purpose are all indicators that students are refining their understanding of main idea. As such, they can see how the main idea helps them "organize the different paragraphs," "pinpoint what is important from what is not," and "put ideas together after reading several books on a topic." Making the process of determining main ideas explicit helps students become more strategic about their reading. It not only gives them moves they can make as readers, but also gives them language to communicate their process, which can help both student and teacher focus on specific areas of confusion. The jump from 9 percent to 30 percent is an important jump, but it is not enough. Such results show that we need to provide more than three weeks of explicit instruction; we need to keep teaching main idea explicitly to all students, and to ELs who struggle with reading in particular.

What Does Identifying Main Ideas Look Like?

Finding the main idea is often challenging. Don't expect students to master this skill quickly; you'll need to repeat the process of modeling, guided practice, and independent practice many times over several weeks. Start with texts that state the main ideas explicitly; for example, "One of the most important achievements of . . . was . . ." and move toward texts that require inferences to determine the main idea. Preview the section you want your students to read and determine the explicitness of the main ideas in those sections (or the need to infer it) and the appropriateness of the text to your students' needs. Figure 5–1 offers some guidance for choosing texts for teaching main ideas.

After selecting texts, there is still a lot of teaching to be done. As we know, finding the main idea in an informational text is often complex, and it is easy for students to get distracted from their purpose. Here is a sample paragraph where students are asked to find the main idea:

> Because they were hunters, Plains tribes were always moving their villages to follow the buffalo herds. For this reason they had homes, called tepees, that they could take down and put back together quickly. Tepees were made by leaning long poles together and covering them with buffalo hides. (*Native Americans* by J. Cipriano, 16)

A student interested in the home types of different Native American tribes might say that the main idea is that Plains Indians lived in tepees that they built with long poles and buffalo hides. However, if our purpose as a class is about geography and climate, we may need to direct the reader back to our guiding questions.

Figure 5–1. Tips for Choosing Texts for Teaching Main Ideas

- Begin with texts in which the main ideas are explicitly stated.
- Choose texts at reading levels that are appropriate to your students' abilities.
- Proceed with texts that require inferring the main idea, and offer lots of modeling and opportunities for guided practice.
- Choose texts featuring a variety of structures (compare/contrast, hierarchical, time or order sequence, descriptive, cause/effect, question/answer) so that they learn how to identify main ideas within varying text structures.
- Select several books suitable for partner or small-group reading so that students find explicit or inferential main ideas based on their needs for comprehension and their topic interests.

We often need to help the reader differentiate between a really interesting tidbit and the main idea of the paragraph that the author is trying to convey (i.e., the nomadic nature of the Plains tribes).

Another way the teacher can refocus students is to make sure the students' background knowledge and personal beliefs and/or experiences don't cloud their ability to find a main idea. Take the paragraph below:

> Hunting buffalo was important for Native Americans living on the Plains. They ate buffalo meat and made clothing from the skin. They used the bones to make tools and weapons, and the horns for cups and spoons. No parts were wasted. Even the cleaned-out stomach was used to carry water. And the tail served as a whip or flyswatter! (*Native Americans* by J. Cipriano, 14)

A student who has a passion for animals and already knows that American buffalo nearly became extinct may interpret the main idea as, "Plains Indians hunted a lot of buffalo, disregarding their survival." This is not a main idea, because the fact that every part of the animal was used indicates that the tribe did not disregard the animal's survival. This is a great opportunity to point out to students how their own perspective can lead to missing what the author is trying to convey as most important. If I had such a conversation in my classroom, I would view this as helpful clarification for the entire class. Differentiating between our biases and what the text says is essential learning. Redirecting students' attention to what idea is most central to the paragraph will help. See Figure 5–2 for other points to help identify main ideas. For more ideas about text and text structures around this specific grade 6 social studies unit of Native Americans, see Figure 5–3.

Figure 5–2. Things to Remember When Identifying Main Ideas

- A main idea is not always the first sentence of a paragraph (i.e., it is not the same as a topic sentence). For example, what sentences contain the central meaning in this paragraph?
- A main idea may be in bold print, begin or end a passage, or refer to an illustration or diagram/graph.
- There may be more than one main idea in a text.
- A main idea is not always explicitly stated. What we need to teach students is that the main idea is the *who* or *what* the paragraph is about (Klingner, Vaugh, and Schumm 1998), and that the main idea is usually repeated, hinted at, or emphasized in most sentences.
- A main idea is often what the author views as the most important thing to convey. This may be different from the student's viewpoint, and it is important to explicitly teach this skill.
- Time sequences have lots of important ideas; identifying some as more important than others may miss the point.
- Not all paragraphs or passages have main ideas; some may be made up only of secondary details.
- Determining what is unimportant or of secondary meaning often helps students to identify relevant information more readily.

Figure 5–3.   Examples of Trade Books for a Unit on Native Americans and Suggested Uses

Book Title and Information	Lexile Level (L)/ Guided Reading Level (GRL)[1]	Suggested Uses	Text Structures
Native Americans, J. Cipriano, Benchmark Education. Pages: 22 ISBN: 9781583449035	800L, GRL: N	**Whole-class lessons** on activating background knowledge, monitoring comprehension, and finding main ideas (mostly inferential) **Content-specific vocabulary for ELs**: *lodges, moccasins, Pueblo, tepee*	Descriptive Compare and Contrast Cause and Effect
The Inuit, K. Cunningham and P. Benoit, Scholastic. Pages: 48 ISBN: 9780531207604	910L	**Small-group reading** in which students activate background knowledge and monitor comprehension (mostly inferential)	Descriptive Compare and Contrast
Native Americans of the Plains, D. Kops, Benchmark Education. Pages: 32 ISBN: 9781410862501	670L, GRL: Q	**Small-group reading** in which students find main ideas (mostly inferential) **Content-specific vocabulary for ELs**: *tepee*	Descriptive Sequential Compare and Contrast
The Iroquois: People of the Northeast, R. Maile, National Geographic. Theme Sets Pages: 30 ISBN: 9780792247289	750L, GRL: S	**Small group reading** in which students find main ideas (mostly inferential) **Content-specific vocabulary for ELs**: *expedition, moccasins, trade*	Descriptive Sequential Compare and Contrast Biographical
The Pueblos: People of the Southwest, R. Maile, National Geographic. Theme Sets Pages: 30 ISBN: 9780792247272	710L, GRL: S	**Small-group reading** in which students find main ideas (both explicit and inferential) **Content-specific vocabulary for ELs**: *moccasins, pueblos, trade*	Descriptive Sequential Compare and Contrast Biographical
The Inuit, A. Santela, Children's Press. Pages: 48 ISBN: 9780516273198	770L, GRL: N	**Small-group reading** in which students find main ideas (mostly explicit)	Descriptive

Figure 5–3. Examples of Trade Books for a Unit on Native Americans and Suggested Uses *(continued)*

Book Title and Information	Lexile Level (L)/ Guided Reading Level (GRL)[1]	Suggested Uses	Text Structures
The Pueblos, A. Flanagan, Children's Press. Pages: 48 ISBN: 9780516206264	940L, GRL: N	**Small-group reading** in which students find main ideas (both explicit and inferential)	Descriptive Compare and Contrast
The Lakota Sioux, A. Santela, Children's Press. Pages: 48 ISBN: 9780516273235	740L, GRL: P	**Small-group reading** in which students activate background knowledge and monitor comprehension (mostly explicit) **Content-specific vocabulary for ELs**: *settlers*	Descriptive Compare and Contrast

[1] Lexile levels range from BR–1600L. Texts are assessed and leveled based on their semantic and syntactic elements. Lexile levels can be found at www.lexile.com. Other leveling systems such as "Guided Reading Level" range from A to Z and take into account text length, layout, structure and organization, illustrations, words, phrases, and sentences, literary features, and content and theme. Guided reading levels can be found at www.scholastic.com/bookwizard. *A note of caution:* Leveling systems are helpful to guide text selection for students of varying reading levels. However, they provide rough "estimates" of a match between the text and the reader. Texts vary in difficulty also in relation to a reader's characteristics, being harder or easier based on support, background knowledge, interest, and so on.

An Instructional Model for Main Idea

As proficient readers, we usually spot the most important ideas in a paragraph or a passage easily. But breaking this process into steps can seem redundant, yet it is essential for our struggling reader ELs. Effective main idea instruction needs to contain the elements shown in Figure 5–4.

Figure 5–4. Elements of Effective Main Idea Instruction

- Model your own thinking about determining importance and how to identify it numerous times, with various types of informational texts (e.g., persuasion, explanation).
- Explicitly teach finding the main idea and determining importance until students gain some self-efficacy with the strategy and feel more comfortable using it independently.
- Model how students can use the text features of different informational texts to help them determine the most important ideas (e.g., some texts may have questions as headings, the answers to which are likely the main ideas).
- Present students with various text structures that help them see the hierarchy between the main ideas and supporting details.
- Present texts that contain main idea(s) in various places within a paragraph or passage so students don't think of the main idea as the topic sentence.
- Provide several texts on the same topic so students see how different authors present the most important ideas. Provide opportunities to reread texts if necessary.

(continues)

Figure 5–4. Elements of Effective Main Idea Instruction *(continued)*

- Have students read one paragraph, page, or section of informational text at a time. Ask them to select words that hint at the main idea. Follow up with supporting details.
- Discuss essential words related to the main idea that are ambiguous or confusing. Ask students to cover up the sentence containing the main idea and lead them to derive what the main idea is.
- Remind and show students that main ideas are not always explicitly stated. Sometimes they are governed by the reader's purpose, prior knowledge/experiences, and author's purpose.
- Provide opportunities to discuss main ideas in groups or pairs.
- Discuss students' selection of main ideas and supporting details as a class.
- Provide practice for main idea(s) identification in the context of other comprehension strategies.

Let's see how these elements play out in instruction. In the instructional seven-step model that follows, you'll see how Shannon teaches main idea and supporting details explicitly to her sixth-grade ELs during her Native American unit.

Step 1. Provide purpose for the strategy.

Shannon begins the lesson by explicitly explaining what the strategy is and what good readers do. She says to her students: "Good readers often think about what is most important in a text. They think about the *who* or *what* in informational texts to see what ideas are more important than others. They also know that reading to find these will probably help them to better understand what they read."

Step 2. Start with a paragraph containing one explicitly stated main idea.

Shannon selects a paragraph that has a clear main idea stated in the first sentence. Since Shannon wants to show her thinking and model inductive reasoning, she covers up the main idea before she shows the paragraph to students. Her intention is to demonstrate that the main idea is repeated, hinted at, or emphasized in most sentences.

Here is the paragraph Shannon projects from *Native Americans,* by J. Cipriano (p.18), with the main idea covered (shaded here):

> Native Americans of the Eastern Woodlands used the natural resources provided by the surrounding forests. The Iroquois (EER-ih-kwoi), who lived in what is now New York State, built homes called wigwams by bending round tress into round shapes. The roof was made of bark and dried grass, or thatch. A small hole let out the smoke from the cooking fires.

She asks the students to listen carefully as she reads the paragraph aloud, noting that there's "something big" missing. She then asks, "What is this paragraph talking about?"

Sarah raises her hand. "What the Iroquois's home was made of."

Shannon pushes Sarah's thinking. "What is it made of?"

Umar shyly volunteers, "Th–th–thatch, trees, bark," reading directly from text.

"Do we know the meaning of *thatch*, Umar?" Shannon encourages.

"It says it there, in the sentence: 'The roof was made of bark and dried grass, or thatch.' It says *or,* so thatch is dry grass and bark, from the trees."

Shannon prompts, "What is another word for all those things?"

"Natural resources," Santiago exclaims.

In this brief exchange Sarah helps her ELs interact closely with the text and think inductively about what the main idea would be.

Step 3. Explain that often there is more than one main idea in a text. Also, the main idea may not always be stated explicitly.

Shannon has led the students to think inductively using the visible information in the text to conclude what the hidden main idea is about. She now uncovers the first sentence of the paragraph and reads it. "Would you say 'Native Americans of the Eastern Woodlands used the natural resources provided by the surrounding forests' is the main idea?" Shannon first led her students with a strong scaffold for what the main idea is in this paragraph, and then she continued by making sure students could see how their previous answers related to the one she provided.

Step 4. Show how supporting details relate to the identified main idea.

Shannon introduces the ideas of supporting details and then gives specific illustrations to make sure students understand both the academic term as well as the specific paragraph details. She says to the class: "Have you heard of supporting details? Supporting details are things that describe or give more information about the main idea."

Shannon points out how the other sentences are details supporting the main idea of natural resources ("wigwams were made by bending young trees," "longhouses were built of bark," etc.). She says, "'Bending dried trees' describes how they used the natural resources."

To reinforce the concepts of main idea and supporting details, she reads another paragraph related to another Native American Tribe. She says, "I'm going to read aloud a paragraph and show you how I think about finding the main idea and supporting details. I'd like you to follow along." She reads the following paragraph:

Women held great power in Iroquois society. They chose the chiefs who became council members, and they could change the decisions made by men. They were also in charge of farming, while men hunted deer, fished, and went to war.

She continues to model her thinking by saying, "When I am looking for the main idea, I'm looking for what most of the sentences are about or relate to. Sometimes I can find the main idea written in the paragraph; sometimes I have to think beyond the paragraph or make an inference. Let me think, what are all these sentences mostly about?" She summarizes her thinking across sentences for her students: "Mmmhh, it seems they are about how powerful women were among the Iroquois; they had different roles and jobs."

After modeling main idea identification, Shannon asks herself (to continue modeling), "Which sentences give us supporting details that support the main idea?" She identifies at least two details that support the main idea she had previously identified: "Women did farming; they also could have roles in government, like councils. These tell me or give me examples of their power." This sequence of modeling—by thinking first for the main idea and then for details—allows students to gain a clearer understanding of the link between the main idea and their supporting details.

Step 5. Provide opportunities for students to display the main idea and supporting details graphically.

After discussing the paragraph on Iroquois women Shannon uses the graphic organizer, completing it while thinking aloud. This think-aloud serves two purposes: (1) it provides explicit instruction on each step of the strategy, and (2) it gives ELs the academic language, syntax, and pronunciation for this task. By repeating this task when they complete their own graphic organizer, students reinforce the strategy and language learning. Shannon then points out that the supporting details in the rest of the sentences in the paragraph relate back to the idea of women's power in Iroquois society, probing for their views on why (see Figure 5–5).

Finding the main idea requires significant practice within and across texts. One way to help establish relevance of the main idea and provide practice is to have students work in small groups to determine the main ideas and supporting details and then place their opinions in a class graphic organizer. From here, the class could debate why readers should care about the main idea. You could use these guiding questions:

- Why is it important for readers to pay attention to main ideas when reading?
- How do they help with reading?

Figure 5–5. A Graphic Organizer Linking Main Idea and Details

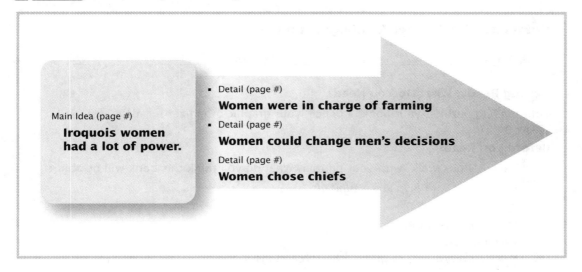

Main Idea (page #)

Iroquois women had a lot of power.

- Detail (page #)
Women were in charge of farming
- Detail (page #)
Women could change men's decisions
- Detail (page #)
Women chose chiefs

Step 6. Have students practice in pairs or small groups.

This step is crucial in Shannon's classroom and is the first big step toward independence. Pair or small-group reading activities give students an opportunity to apply what they learned during the whole-class lesson in books they can read with some, but not continuous, support. ELs in particular reap the benefits of working in small groups or pairs if the tasks are text-based, have clear goals, and require high-order, critical thinking.

In our own work with grades 6 and 7 ELs, including Shannon's students, we provided written guidelines regarding how to handle roles in partner reading through specific directions (see Figure 5–6), with student pairs taking turns reading assigned text sections, one partner asking questions after reading and both rereading silently before attempting to answer their partners' questions and identify main ideas. Questions had to follow adequate use of question words and, when possible, correct use of English for forming questions (e.g., verb position) versus forming main idea statements. Poster guidelines provided support for these language dimensions so ELs could focus more on the content of their questions while having extra support for question forms and main idea statements (and).

By providing specific guidelines, we helped students set clear expectations and opportunities for extended reading for each partner/group member.

Figure 5–6.

Guidelines for Partner Reading: Main Idea

Book Title _____   **Author** _____

Getting Ready: What Do You Need?

Your reading partner, your book, a pencil, your graphic organizer for main idea, and sticky notes

Before You Read

1. Take a "book walk" with your partner. What do you think this book will be about?

    Use C.H.I.P.S. to help you. Think of:

    C = Chapter titles
    H = Headings/subtitles
    I = Index/glossary
    P = Pictures/maps/diagrams/charts/captions
    S = Special vocabulary

    Discuss with each other: What is your purpose for reading this book?

Reading Text Together and Asking Questions

2. Decide who will read each of the assigned pages aloud.

3. First, silently read the pages that you will read aloud to your partner. If you are struggling with a word, ask your partner. If your partner doesn't know, check the glossary and/or raise your hand and ask your teacher.

4. Take turns reading your assigned pages to each other. Be sure to read the pages in order.

5. While you are reading, record any new vocabulary on a sticky note.

6. Each of you, choose a paragraph or page to select main idea and supporting details. Enter these in your main idea organizer.

7. Share the main ideas and details with each other.

After Reading

8. After reading, add new information to your graphic organizer. Remember that today you are focusing on the main idea and supporting details.

9. Explain why this is the main idea(s) and how the details support it.

10. Discuss any questions you have about the sections read. Think and discuss how your questions relate to your purpose for reading this text.

Step 7. Give students lots of time to practice independently.

Students need time to practice new strategies on their own. During the initial focus on main idea, have students use Figure 5–7. They can use Figure 5–6 after they've spent four or five days delving into main ideas and determining importance in various types of texts. Angie, one of Shannon's sixth-grade EL students, responded with this after having used "Becoming a Main Idea Detective" over four days: "After using our 'Becoming a Main Idea Detective' I felt much better about thinking what is important and mostly repeated or hinted at in the paragraph. Before then, I did not know what 'hinted at' meant. Now I see it . . . it's that idea that is referred to, kind of there, but sometimes hidden, and that you need to make sense of what you're reading."

Establishing Relevance

Establishing relevance for tasks and skills is key to motivating students so they persist with challenging tasks, such as main idea identification. When students feel that teachers support their autonomy through a task, they are likely to value and feel positive about it (Grolnick, Ryan, and Deci 1991; Grolnick and Ryan 1989). As a result, they become more engaged with their school tasks (e.g., Connell 1990; Ryan 1993).

There are different ways in which teachers can support students' autonomy for learning. One example of autonomy-supportive teaching is to explain how the topic relates to students' lives and future goals; it is also referred to among

Figure 5–7.

Becoming a Main Idea Detective

1. Ask yourself: *What is this paragraph mostly about? OR, What is the most general or significant statement in this paragraph?*
2. Go back and reread each sentence.
3. Ask yourself: *What seems to be repeated, hinted at, or emphasized in most sentences?*
   a. If you CANNOT figure it out, you have to infer the main idea.
      i. Think of each sentence in the paragraph as a factor in an addition problem in math. Try to figure out what the sentences add up to:

      (A sentence) + (A sentence) + (A sentence) = Main idea

      ii. Ask yourself: *Is there a general statement that applies to most of these ideas? Do other sentences point to or hint at these ideas?*
4. After you identify the main idea, find how the rest of the sentences in the paragraph support that main idea. These are your details!

motivation researchers, as *establishing* or *fostering relevance* (e.g., Assor, Kaplan, and Roth 2002; Black and Deci 2000). For example, let's consider Maria, a sixth-grade student who wants to improve her oral reading. As it turns out, Maria wants to study theater and is already involved in the theater club after school, but she does not enjoy oral reading. Maria is likely to feel more autonomous as she learns how to read fluently after her teacher explains to her that oral fluent reading would greatly enhance her acting skills. To foster relevance, we need to help students see the connection between specific tasks and their interests and goals, current or future.

We do not establish relevance by choosing activities that the teacher deems interesting to the students. That's a guessing game, and it usually results in superficial engagement and learning. Rather, fostering relevance refers to students' understanding the reasons for learning certain skills or topics. Establishing relevance can be done in any discipline and for any content. Let's first explore how we can establish relevance for reading skills, such as comprehension strategies.

Fostering Relevance for Strategy Use

Reminding students of the purpose of a strategy is an essential foundation to teaching students how to use it and to ensuring that they believe it's worth holding on to that teaching. To introduce the purpose for finding main ideas, you can start by asking students to explain this simple question: "Why do we care about finding the main idea in a paragraph or page?" Invite students to think through the "why" and not just be satisfied with answers that relate to "doing well on the test" or "because my teacher says it's what I need to do." Guide the discussion so students think through the need for and process of sifting through information and finding key ideas, how it is easier to remember information instead of just reading every word with the same level of attention. Ideally, students will come to understand that finding main ideas helps with learning and retaining information. After this discussion, present them with the opposite scenario: "What would it be like if I read informational texts, online or offline, without prioritizing information? How would I know what is important and what is not? How would my knowledge be organized? How would I manage to remember information and apply it later?" These discussions will help students begin to realize that comprehending the main idea can help with relevance and prioritizing information.

Another way of establishing relevance is to offer students an explicit description of the strategy and when and how it should be used—which, if you recall from

Chapters 2 and 3, is the first step in the revised gradual release of responsibility model proposed by Duke and colleagues (2011). We need to share with students that good readers often think about what is important in text, and that they try to understand what is important to the author and how she conveys this important information. By doing this we are, in a way, providing a rationale, an explanation, for why identifying the main idea is useful, important, and helpful. We are establishing relevance!

Fostering Relevance for Content Knowledge

Although all students have their favorite and least-favorite school subjects, there are some subjects that tend to be less popular than others. Social studies, and history in particular, does not have the best reputation among late elementary and middle school students. In fact, researchers have shown that many students perceive social studies classes as dull, monotonous, and irrelevant (Chiodo and Byford 2004). In one of the earliest surveys regarding student attitudes toward social studies, researchers found that students in the secondary grades described social studies as having little relevance to their future, as confusing, and as having less importance than other core subjects such as English and mathematics (Fernandez, Massey, and Dornbusch 1976). Even though some high-school students see the value of social studies in gaining an understanding of the political process and civic duties and responsibilities (e.g., Chiodo and Byford 2004), these views seems to change by demographic group, with Caucasian and African American students preferring social studies over other schools subjects, and Hispanic students preferring social studies the least (Corbin 1997). This is not surprising if one thinks that, for most Hispanic ELs, American history taught in the elementary and middle schools is often removed from their own past history and cultures. When faced with this lack of interest in social studies, and history in particular, we worked with middle school teachers on the USHER project to support their students' interests and, ultimately, motivation to read history texts, through establishing relevant activities.

Teachers created inspiring relevance-fostering activities to teach U.S. history, such as visits to local museums and Civil War battlefields, political candidate debates, and campaigns for civil rights. One such relevance-fostering activity that I particularly liked for the Native Americans unit involved inviting to the school a teacher's grandfather who belonged to the Pueblo tribe near Santa Fe, New Mexico. Sixth graders had prepared an extensive list of questions about tribe lifestyle, type of current clothing, foods, shelter/housing, territorial rights, main sources of income, and the extent to which their arts and crafts were preserved and continued today. Although most of the students' questions reflected their curiosity about tribal life today, they were strongly informed by their reading about the history of Native Americans. Students then did additional reading to compare the tribe's present life to their history and generated new questions based on their comparisons. They created an informative display of their knowledge to share with the rest of the school and post in the school library. Two school librarians then helped students communicate, via email and Skype, with members of two other tribes to expand their understanding of tribal culture. Their initial reading kept its momentum through multiple projects and interactions and probably is still carried by those students today. Establishing relevance is the initial burst of energy that creates learning momentum.

Using Guiding, Open-Ended Questions to Foster Content Relevance

Open-ended, guiding questions that can be answered in multiple ways throughout a theme or unit are great tools for holding onto relevance throughout content instruction. The use of guiding, open-ended questions creates a context for extended learning about the topic that goes beyond the immediate learning of the day (see Figure 5–8). When students know that these guiding, open-ended questions are part of their work today, tomorrow, and next week, they have additional context for relevance. They can see that they are working on broad knowledge building, and that the reading of a single text serves a larger purpose. Different from student-generated questions to be discussed in Chapter 6, open-ended questions are generally framed by the teacher and/or curriculum developers. This is because these questions have to be encompassing enough to alert students to several subtopics within a broader topic or unit. For example, let's look at how Gladys White, a social studies and language arts teacher, used open-ended guiding questions for her sixth graders. Here, she reads the guiding questions posted on the bulletin board:

"In which areas did the Native Americans live?

How did geography and climate affect the way Native American tribes met their basic needs?"

Gladys lets students know that for the next two weeks they will read several sets of books on Native Americans and demonstrate their knowledge of Native

Americans by returning to these guiding questions multiple times as they gain new knowledge. She reminds her students that tasks such as finding the main idea and supporting details of one text serve the larger purpose of helping them learn about Native American tribes' ways of living and adaptations to their environment. Although this topic was part of the state curricula and not chosen by students (most topics in the middle and high school are not), having open, guiding questions allows students to see the "bigger picture" of a topic and discuss it in terms of its relevance to other topics and their own lives. Guiding questions can be posed for units in any content area (see Guthrie 2008 for multiple examples). Figure 5–8 shows a few examples of open-ended questions, and tips for generating them, for American history.

Figure 5–8. Tips for Generating Guiding, Open-Ended Questions

- Keep guiding questions open-ended and applicable to several topics within a unit.
- Post these questions in a visible place.
- Remind students of these questions every time they participate in a reading activity.
- Encourage students to enter partial answers to these questions each day.
- Help students find answers to their questions across sources and texts.
- Encourage students to record the page numbers and source names for their answers.

Examples of open-ended, guiding questions:

- Native American tribes: How did geography and climate affect the way American Indian groups met their basic needs?
- Colonial America: How was each American colony influenced by its geography and people?
- European exploration: Why did European countries compete for power in North America?
- Gold Rush: What was life like for the Gold Rush pioneers?
- Immigration: What was life like in the tenements? How did the Progressive Movement affect the lives of different groups of immigrants?
- World War I: What were the initial sentiments toward WWI in Europe? Why? What were the sentiments toward WWI in the United States? Why?

Reminder: Pair Motivation Practices with Comprehension Strategies (It Doesn't Matter Which)

The pairings of a reading strategy with a motivational practice in Chapters 3 through 7 are only examples of potential pairings; one could easily pair different practices with strategies or multiple ones. However, identifying main ideas and fostering relevance often work best when done together. If we only teach identifying the main idea and supporting details of an informational text without situating the reading of the text in a context that's relevant for our EL readers, then "important" can too easily become a symbol of what the teacher deems important instead of the author's main idea or an idea that is important as reached by consensus. When we pay attention to who our EL students are—reminding them that the purpose of identifying the main idea is to help them grow as readers such that they build knowledge from text—we show them that reading informational texts for content-area learning really matters.

6

Text-Based Questioning and Autonomy

Wanting to Know More

Curiosity is an innate trait that is somewhat blunted by experience and context. In the anxiety over coverage, some teachers argue that they don't have time for student curiosity because it invites too many surprise tangents into instruction, and those tangents bite into the limited time most teachers have. This anxiety is heightened for teachers of ELs because we so desperately want ELs to reach the same level of achievement as their non-EL peers. There is so much catching up to do! But we can't teach children without nourishing their desire to know. We just can't. If you struggle with this, it's probably only because you haven't seen enough effective models. If we want our students to be curious, to know more, then we need to provide daily experiences that invite them to be so. In this chapter we'll explore how student questioning can foster autonomy and the desire to know more through informational texts.

The Learner Needs to Choose: Why Autonomy Is Essential for ELs

Children are naturally curious about the world and what happens in it, and informational texts appeal to that curiosity (Doiron 1994; Ness 2013). Helping your ELs want to read more informational texts means giving them some choices. As human beings, we can never experience total freedom—limits are part of human life. This makes the freedoms we do have important. Like other psychological needs, autonomy is best understood when it's constrained. For example, there is much discussion, and rightly so, about the negative impact on limiting teacher autonomy. When your ability to decide how and what you will teach is severely constrained, you resent those limits. These limits communicate a lack of faith in your decision-making, which can make it more difficult to teach. Many teachers leave the profession because of this.

These larger human issues of motivation play out in the classroom. Consider how limiting autonomy affects ELs' identities as readers. When we tell students what they *have to* read, we are also telling them that what they *can't* read. If we want students to become lifelong readers, they need to make choices about their own reading lives. Unfortunately, most school-related reading is assigned with an understanding that students will be rewarded if they complete it and punished if they don't. It is unusual for a student to take on an assignment because he believes it will be enjoyable or challenging. Rather, school-related reading is mostly extrinsically driven; students act based on the punishments or rewards for the behavior rather than the behavior itself. We don't want human beings to do good only because they are afraid of the consequences of doing bad or because they want the recognition of doing well. That kind of system only creates compliance or defiance, not autonomy. Having activities exclusively led by extrinsic motivation is not effective in healthy identity formation, let alone learning. We can provide pizza points to students to read during a specific moment in time, but we can't make them love reading and we certainly can't force children to become lifelong readers. Instead, we have to offer them ongoing, compelling invitations to read. To qualify as compelling, the invitation to read must involve some student autonomy.

Letting students choose what they can read is an important part of our invitation to autonomy, yet sometimes the element of choice has to be restricted. When we're teaching a given topic, such as global warming or the Revolutionary War, we have to cover certain essential content, so we can't decide to skip climate change or the Boston Tea Party. In these learning situations, we need to identify informational texts that discuss concepts related to that topic in a compelling way, with the depth that students need. Yet even in situations like this, the opportunity for choice and student autonomy exists.

As we discussed in Chapter 1, autonomy support can take more than one form. We can support autonomy by acknowledging the importance of students' opinions and feelings by explaining the relevance of schoolwork, and by providing choices. Offering students meaningful academic choices is one of the most widely used practices. One way we can extend the positive power of choices is through teaching text-based questioning.

What Does Text-Based Questioning Look Like?

The strategy of text-based questioning is an effective way of fostering a sense of autonomy and choice in struggling reader ELs. Text-based questioning is the practice of identifying questions that you, as a reader, ask before, during, and after your reading. In other words, we are not talking about teacher-created questions for a text. A text-based question functions like a personal goal for reading. Students need to know that it is not only normal but also helpful to ask questions throughout the process of reading. By being encouraged to ask questions, students increase their own sense of curiosity about a topic. They increase their success at reading because questions allow them to focus attention on one portion of a text at a time. And, most importantly, they deepen their knowledge when we help them ask questions of increasing complexity (from factual/simple to more conceptual/complex).

All these actions are driven by choice: students control their reading by pursuing their own interests within a curricular topic through their questions (Taboada and Guthrie 2004); they can express novel ideas (Chin and Osborne 2010; Therrien, Wickstrom, and Jones 2006); they can articulate what they do and do not understand (Therrien et al. 2006). We further honor students' autonomy when we post their questions along with their name so that they see that there is value in their thinking for others, as fourth grader Juan describes here:

> "I liked it [asking questions] 'cause people could answer my questions and I could answer theirs. I could learn what they were learning about . . . and they could learn what I was learning about. We learned from each other because we all had questions, we could take a peek into each other's thinking. Also, if the teacher is the one who always asks the questions, then we only gotta learn what she's thinking about and that's not our own thinking."

Student text-based questioning helps students like Juan see that while they might not know all the content or comprehend all the text, they can ask the right kinds of questions that will help them learn more from their reading.

When we use text-based questioning, we ask students to pose their own questions about a text *before, while,* and *after* reading a text. Students can generate questions through talk or writing. It is usually helpful for students to record their questions so that they can refer back to them during and after reading. If you want students to share their questions with each other, they could write them down on a sticky note or a classroom poster. If your goal is for students to share how questions helped them better understand the key ideas in the text, perhaps sharing them through talk suffices. The important thing to keep in mind is that questions need to be linked directly to the text to increase the chances of getting them answered. As we teach question generation as a strategy, students also incorporate other reading strategies to inform their work.

- They use text clues, such as the section heading (Berkeley and Riccomini 2013).
- They preview the first sentence (often the topic sentence) of the paragraph.
- They activate their prior knowledge about the topic to predict.
- They summarize the paragraph in an effort to answer their question (Berkeley and Riccomini 2013).

As we do this work, we remind students that skilled readers are active readers, readers who ask questions about a text.

A good way to help struggling reader ELs learn to ask text-based questions is to highlight text components, such as important ideas or topic sentences. By asking students to think about important ideas of the text they are (1) working on a previously learned comprehension strategy (identification of main idea or relevant ideas), and (2) drafting a question that is based on the important information contained in the text. However, this is just one way to approach student text-based questioning. Question generation does not always have to be linked to main idea. What counts is to get ELs into a *questioning mode* about text. Given that most ELs are not used to an inquisitive stance, this is a first good step. ELs need to understand that their questions don't have to be about *the* idea or *one* main idea, but rather about information that seems important to them within a section of the text.

We can model this strategy by projecting a paragraph on the board and then direct students to read along as you read the paragraph aloud. Conduct a think-aloud to demonstrate how you find an important idea in a paragraph. Write the important idea for all to see. If some details related to it are important to note, write those too. Then ask a question about the important idea and/or the details. Write your question down so students "see" your thinking. Remind students that good readers ask questions about important information as they read. The diagram shown in Figure 6–1 can help show the sequence of your thinking. It is a visual example of a think-aloud that helps students understand how to ask a text-based question. Be metacognitive about questioning; that is, discuss how questions help focus our attention when reading and help us think more carefully about what we read.

Figure 6–1. Visual example to model a way to ask a text-based question

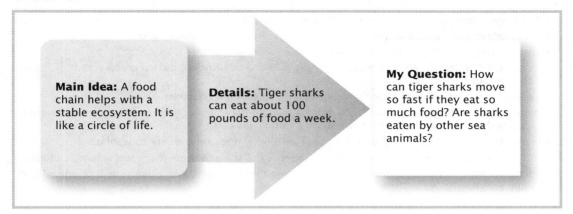

Note that in Figure 6–1 the questions asked are not about the main idea, they are tangential to it. This is because, as noted earlier, the goal is to get the students into *questioning mode,* so it is a good idea not to lead them exclusively toward main idea or important idea questions. Let them ask! Refining the type of questions can be done in due time, after they become stronger at text-based question asking.

As students begin to learn the skill of text-based questions, it is also important to make sure we choose the right texts so the questions can get answered. Many teachers share the challenge expressed by fifth-grade teacher Myriam: "If I teach my students to ask questions but those questions do not get answered, the motivational aspect of questioning gets lost. I also fail to reach my goal of increasing comprehension." This is why we need to keep questions text-based and to choose the right kinds of informational texts for students to do this work.

Informational texts share specific information and support concept development (Pappas 2006), prompting both factual and conceptual questions. They also have unique structures and text features—diagrams, photos, captions, topic sentences, subheadings—that help students activate relevant background knowledge. Unlike narrative—where a character in a story can be connected to a child's own experiences, allowing the child to expand upon ideas in the story that are not always explicit in the text (e.g., how do you think Joey feels about having lost his puppy?)—informational texts include facts and technical vocabulary that prompt types and levels of questions that can potentially be answered by the text. However, if we want students to engage in these kind of interactions, we need to show them how. Figure 6–2 shows some practices that will encourage your students to become more active, engaged questioners.

Figure 6–2. Supporting Student Text-Based Questioning

- Model your own questions during read-alouds or in small groups.
- Post student questions, with student names next to them, on classroom walls.
- Ensure that questions posted get answered and are renewed often.
- Teach question levels. Model one at a time, and follow with sufficient guided practice and opportunities for independent practice.
- Encourage students to move their questions up the question-level ladder.
- Allow time, at least a day per unit, for students to bring books about their most interesting/favorite topics within the unit; they can ask questions and find answers to them.
- Invite students to discuss their questions with each other and find answers collaboratively.
- Pair up or group students with similar interests so they can share their questions and answers on topics.
- Encourage students to share their questions beyond the classroom, with other school personnel and family members.

Teach Question Forms

In addition to establishing structures that promote text-based questioning, we also need to teach specific types of questions. Questioning strategies for narrative texts have been in use for awhile. For example, some three decades ago, researchers taught struggling readers to ask and answer "wh" questions (e.g., who, what, when, where, why) (Clark, Deshler, Schumaker, Alley, and Warner 1984). Using "who, what, when, where, which, how, and why" question words helps struggling readers remember what questions to ask, which in turn improves comprehension (Faggella-Luby, Schumaker, and Deshler 2007). The teaching of "wh" questions is especially helpful for ELs who struggle with question forms and question structure. For instance, many ELs with beginning levels of English proficiency are likely to recurrently resort to questions starting with "Is" "Are" and "Does." This restricts them to "yes/no" answers, thus limiting the breadth and scope of knowledge they can build from text. The teaching of "wh" question words can be especially helpful to expand their repertoire of questions and answers. Also, teaching ELs to frame their questions with "wh" helps them with learning about alternative syntax structure for question asking. The use of symbols to indicate question words is helpful because memory triggers the meaning of each question word (e.g., *where* generally indicates location, *when* indicates time, etc.) and potential answers to student questions (see Figure 6–3).

Teach a Variety of Question Types

Although researchers have discussed question types and levels for a while now, the use of levels to help students think in terms of essential concepts within

Figure 6–3. Use of Symbols for Prompting the Use of Question Words

Question Word	Symbol
Who?	
What?	
Where?	
When?	
Why?	

informational text is less known among content-area teachers. The usefulness of question levels (see Figure 6–4) is twofold. First, students as young as grade 3 were able to closely think about the content of their questions based on the potential answers. As a result, the process deepened students' comprehension of science texts and ecological science concepts (Taboada and Guthrie 2004). Further, we also found that ELs increased their comprehension of social studies texts through the process of question generation (Taboada, Buehl, and Richie 2013). There are four levels of questions that can help build complexity for students. See Figures 6–5 and 6–6 for examples of question levels in science and social studies, respectively.

By categorizing questions into levels, or types, we can help students broaden their repertoire of questions and become aware of the variety of information presented by a text. Each level identifies the kind of information being requested by the question. For example, a level one question asks for simple factual information: "How many teeth do sharks have?" Yet, a level 3 question requires an

Figure 6–4. Levels of Questions

Level One: Factual Information
These questions are a request for a simple answer, such as a single fact or yes/no answer.

Level Two: Simple Explanation
These questions are a request for a simple explanation about a core concept identified for the unit or theme.

Level Three: Complex Explanation
These questions probe for core concepts by using specific prior knowledge within the question.

Level Four: Pattern Relationships
These questions ask about relationships among ideas or key concepts across books and topics.

Figure 6–5. Question Levels in Science

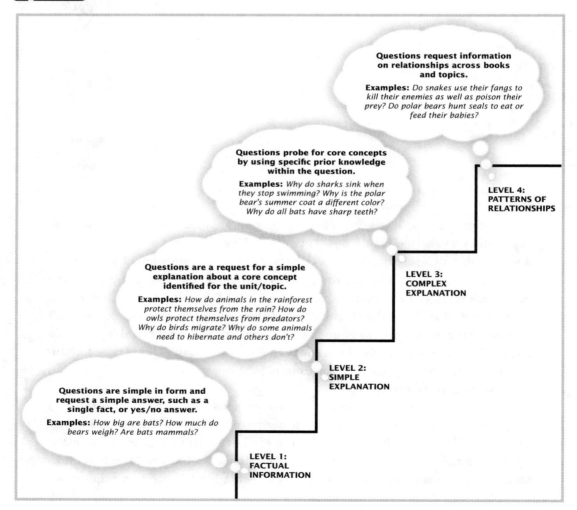

Figure 6–6. Question Levels in Social Studies

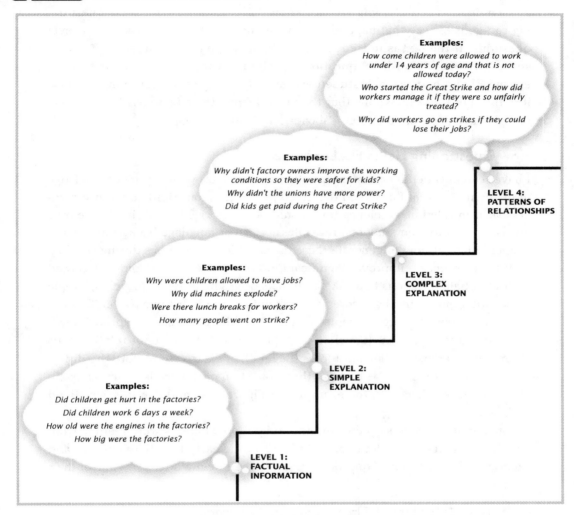

Examples:

How come children were allowed to work under 14 years of age and that is not allowed today?

Who started the Great Strike and how did workers manage it if they were so unfairly treated?

Why did workers go on strikes if they could lose their jobs?

LEVEL 4: PATTERNS OF RELATIONSHIPS

Examples:

Why didn't factory owners improve the working conditions so they were safer for kids?

Why didn't the unions have more power?

Did kids get paid during the Great Strike?

LEVEL 3: COMPLEX EXPLANATION

Examples:

Why were children allowed to have jobs?

Why did machines explode?

Were there lunch breaks for workers?

How many people went on strike?

LEVEL 2: SIMPLE EXPLANATION

Examples:

Did children get hurt in the factories?

Did children work 6 days a week?

How old were the engines in the factories?

How big were the factories?

LEVEL 1: FACTUAL INFORMATION

explanation that demonstrates conceptual knowledge: "How can tiger sharks move so fast if they eat so much food?"

We can use these categories to assess how students engage with a text. If ELs are generating simple level one questions, it might be an indicator that they don't yet know how to ask deeper questions, or that their comprehension is at the factual level only. However, we should not assume that low-level questions are an indicator of poor comprehension and simply give ELs an easier text; lower expectations are too often the experience of ELs that keep them trapped in low achievement. The only way we can know for certain how far their questioning can go is to see what happens when we encourage them to ask higher-level questions. If the text is indeed too hard, then we give them an easier text but still encourage higher-level questioning. The most important thing is that we engage ELs in higher-level, student-generated, text-based questioning because it is through these questions that they can deepen their text-based knowledge (Scardamalia and Bereiter 1992; Taboada and Guthrie 2004).

How Questioning Helps ELs Learn More

I have seen how depth of student questioning correlates with depth of knowledge in my own research. I observed that the types of questions third and fourth graders asked in relation to science texts could be categorized according to the four levels, and that when students, regardless of age or language background, were explicitly taught how to generate these different level questions during reading, their comprehension improved significantly. From grades 3 to 7, students learned to differentiate questions that ask about facts or yes/no answers (Level 1), simple explanation questions about core concepts within a unit or topic (Level 2), questions that probe for core concepts within a topic by using specific prior knowledge within the question (Level 3), and questions that ask about relationships among ideas across books and topics (Level 4). A clear way to note the differences between the levels is through the application of the levels to actual examples. Please refer again to the examples in Figures 6–5 and 6–6 in science and social studies.

In a grade 6 social studies unit on immigration, students were reading from a variety of texts on the topic of child labor in the early twentieth century and generated all four levels of questions. Here, in their own words, are some of their questions:

- Level 1: "Did the children get hurt in the factories?"
- Level 2: "Why were children allowed to have jobs?"
- Level 3: "Why didn't factory owners improve the working conditions so they were safer for kids?"
- Level 4: "How come children were allowed to work under fourteen years of age and that is not allowed today?"

As you can see, the act of self-directed questioning teaches students that reading an informational text is an act of acquiring content knowledge while it deepens comprehension. We cannot expect ELs to acquire content knowledge without this kind of active questioning. In my research, those students who tended to ask lower-level text-based questions were consistently weaker in their comprehension than those students who asked higher-level questions. Furthermore, those students asking higher-level questions were better able to explain the key concepts within text. They could discuss mammals' adaptations rather than just list body features. They could discuss slavery as a condition of human life rather than just name the states that had slavery before the Civil War. These findings were similar whether the students were English native speakers or ELs (Taboada and Guthrie 2004; Taboada, Bianco, and Bowerman 2012). Clearly, teaching question levels to ELs works and is essential instruction to ensure our EL students' success both as readers and learners in all the content areas.

The FIST Strategy

In addition to teaching students to ask questions before, during, and after reading, we can teach them how to keep their questions grounded in the text. For example, students can use the topic or the first sentence of a paragraph to generate a question that guides their reading. Although first sentences are not always the main idea or topic sentence, they generally carry useful information. We can prompt students to read the first sentence of a paragraph and create a question from the sentence that might be answered by the paragraph, read the paragraph, and then determine whether the author answered the question or not. This self-questioning strategy known as FIST (First, Indicate, Search, Tie) (adopted from Clark et al. 1984) is described in Figure 6–7.

The focus of FIST on small specifics in a text—the first sentence in a paragraph—helps EL struggling readers who frequently feel overwhelmed by the sea of detail in an informational text. After the EL has asked a question, s/he can read the rest of the paragraph to determine whether their question can be answered or not. See Figure 6–8 for a model of the explicit instruction.

Figure 6–7. The FIST Strategy: Asking and Answering Text-Based Questions

F: Read the first sentence in the paragraph.

I: Indicate a question based on information in the first sentence.

S: Search for the answer to the question.

T: Tie the answer to the question with a paraphrase.

Figure 6–8. Instructional Model of the FIST Strategy

Teacher Directions	"Use the FIST strategy as you read. When you reach the FI, ask a question about the first sentence. When you see ST, look back at the paragraph for answers. Then tie the answers into the question in one sentence. If the paragraph doesn't answer the question, ask a new question that the paragraph does answer."
Sample Paragraph with Directions and Embedded FIST Strategy:	
FI. The S.S. Edmund Fitzgerald was a freighter that hauled iron and taconite ore from the western end of the Great Lakes to the steel factories in Detroit, Michigan. The freighter had left the port in Superior, Wisconsin, slightly ahead of the Arthur M. Anderson. When an early November storm produced high waves and gale-force winds, the two ships maintained close contact. **ST.**	
Sample Student Question(s) (FI)	"What did the freighter do?" "Where did the freighter leave?" "What is a freighter?"
Sample Student Summary Sentence (ST)	"It left the port and there was a big storm." "In lake Superior." "It did not answer my question, but I think I know it's a big ship."
Sample Retell Responses	"It's about ships that lost contact in a storm."

Adapted from Manset-Williamson, Dunn, Hinshaw, and Nelson (2008)

Parsing the text and getting students to ask a question about the first sentence limits the amount of text and keeps students' focus on question asking for a short amount of text. This is helpful for most struggling readers, but it is especially helpful for struggling reader ELs. Similarly, asking students to go back to the text for explicit answers and ask a new question if answers are not found in the text makes students re-read, which is a useful fix-up strategy that we discuss in Chapter 8.

Collaborative Use of Questioning

Collaborative practice is an essential way of building ELs' capacity for asking questions. Different from modeling your thinking, now you think *with* the students. Instead of the "I do" of modeling, collaborative practice entails the "We do." You may recall from Chapter 2 that, different from guided practice (when students respond to the strategy in a more individual way), collaborative practice is an intermediate step between modeling and guided practice when students apply the strategy to new portions of text, together with the teacher. Like guided practice, collaborative use of the strategy works when the task you give students needs to be similar to the one you modeled. Next, we'll look at a few of my favorite ways to scaffold by asking questions through collaborative practice.

R.I.C.H., A Scaffolding Tool

R.I.C.H. is a question-asking scaffolding tool developed by former social studies teacher Leila Richie Nuland who collaborated on the USHER research project. R.I.C.H. stands for the steps that lead students to use text to ask questions:

1. **R**ead the passage.
2. **I**dentify important idea/s and supporting details.
3. **C**reate a question.
4. Think: **H**ow can I answer the question?

In our research, R.I.C.H. worked especially well with middle school ELs (e.g., Taboada Barber, Richey, and Buehl 2013) because the steps/letters in the mnemonic help them automatize the use of text-based questioning. Figure 6–9 shows an instructional model of the tool.

Remember that the goal during guided practice is to get students to work more independently with the strategy while you are still scaffolding their application or use of the strategy. You may want to conclude guided practice by emphasizing

Figure 6–9. Collaborative Practice of R.I.C.H.

- Remind students of the purpose of text-based questioning.
- Review the R.I.C.H. mnemonic with students. Explain that R.I.C.H. will help them ask text-based questions. Ensure that all students have the text accessible to them.
- Let students read along. Direct students to follow along silently as you read a passage or short section. Point out that you are going to "read the passage," which is the first step in R.I.C.H.
- After reading, you can indicate, "Now I would like you to help me find an important idea and supporting details." Point to the "I" in R.I.C.H. for identifying important ideas. Encourage students to share ideas, and write a few down for all to see.

Guided Practice
- Next, you can point out to the "C" in R.I.C.H. by stating, "Now I would like you to help me create a question about the important ideas." Write down some of the students' questions.
- After creating a question, point to the "H" in R.I.C.H. and ask, "How am I going to answer the question?" Direct students to review the text again as you point out the sections of text that answer some, if not all, of their questions.

that *students* generate good student questions (rather than the teacher) to help them with reading, saying:

> **Guided practice:** "I have called Juan and Maria together to work on asking questions while you read the (frog) book and other books. After every few pages I will ask each of you to stop and ask a question using R.I.C.H. We will talk about your questions and then read on to see if we can answer them. My goal is for you to become so comfortable with using R.I.C.H. that, eventually, you will not need it and will ask questions on your own *before* and *during* reading."

Develop Independence

How many questions, or even what kind or quality of questions, students generate is not the final assessment of this strategy. We need to confirm that students understand and can transfer this to different contexts. We need to know that students not only can generate the questions but also use them to make meaning of a text. The text may not fully or even partially answer every student-generated question; in fact, those incomplete answers can help drive students to want to read and learn more. But ELs need to see that the act of generating their own question serves a purpose: it helps make them smarter about the world and stronger readers.

There are many ways to offer ELs opportunities for independent questioning. When I do this work with students, *initially* I provide a reference resource of the tool, like a bookmark of the R.I.C.H. mnemonic and/or a graphic organizer that facilitates independent use or application of the steps previously learned. Students can practice in small groups or pairs first, and then individually. Figure 6–10 offers some suggestions on fostering independence.

Figure 6–10. Scaffolding ELs Toward Independent Text-based Questioning

- Lead students to read either a teacher-selected or a self-selected portion of text. (Ensure that these are of roughly the same length across students if you opt for the latter.)
- After students finish reading, have students follow the steps in R.I.C.H. as described above in the Guided Practice section.
- While students complete the steps in R.I.C.H., have them record their ideas and questions in an organized way so they can share these later. The diagram shown in Figure 6–1 used for modeling and guided practice should work well for this purpose.
- Encourage application of the strategy across texts of different lengths and difficulty.
- Provide specific feedback when needed.
- Check for understandings! Independent practice is still part of learning, so student questions and teacher feedback are encouraged.

As you may surmise, I emphasized that I *initially* opted for using similar tools during guided practice as part of the independent practice stage. Ultimately, our goal is for students to feel secure enough in the use of the strategy that they do not need R.I.C.H. or other tools/prompts to support the creation of their text-based questions. This is our end goal: for all students, and especially struggling reader ELs, to develop a way of thinking about using comprehension strategies with informational text that becomes second nature to them.

Let ELs Know Their Questions Are Worth Answering

Asking questions is a critical thinking skill beyond the reading of informational texts. It is the essential way we talk back to the endless flow of information that invades our daily lives. It is a way of pausing and asserting ourselves by evaluating and synthesizing the truth and helpfulness of information. When we teach our ELs how to generate their own text-based questions about an informational text about alligators (see Figure 6–11), the task is greater than the specific text, *Alligators in the Wild*. We can tell our student, particularly an EL who may have a

Figure 6–11. Question asked by Juan, a fourth grader, during the animals adaptations unit.

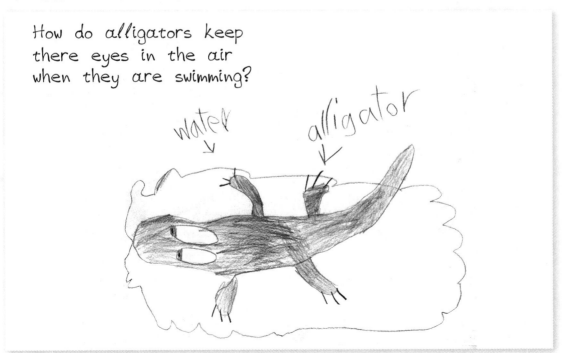

fragile self-efficacy for reading, that not only is a text interesting enough for him to ask questions, but his questions are interesting and worthy enough to talk back to the text. When we honor a student's identity and ideas by encouraging him to express them via his questions, we are engaging the student and supporting him in building autonomy. In our experience, encouraging question asking in effective ways is one way to build autonomous learning. Too often, question asking and autonomy support are overlooked for ELs, because asking questions could mean calling attention to all they do not know. Real joy and learning can happen when we let students know that asking questions is a way of showing their interesting thinking, and is an essential way to learn and grow as readers! Our goal is for students to understand that although they may not have the answer to a question right now, they can choose what to ask and what to focus on by questioning and reading in their quest to find that answer!

Monitoring Comprehension and Collaborating

Determining What We Know

Knowing what we don't know can provide the momentum to learn what tools and resources we need for doing so. But for many ELs, attempting to read informational texts seems to point out their knowledge gaps, especially if they are able to decode the text but lack the background knowledge or vocabulary to understand key concepts. It is easy to empathize with the despair that leads them to complain, "I know what the words mean but I still don't understand!"

Even proficient readers experience confusion with some texts and topics. For example, read this short passage:

> In the late 1800s, physicist Max Planck sought to discover the reason that radiation from a glowing body changes in color from red, to orange, and, finally, to blue as its temperature rises. He found that by making the assumption that energy existed in individual units in the same way that matter does, rather than just as a constant electromagnetic wave—as had been formerly assumed—and was therefore quantifiable, he could find the answer to his question. The existence of these units became the first assumption of quantum theory. In quantum physics, you encounter the Heisenberg uncertainty principle, which says that the better you know the position of a particle, the less you know the momentum, and vice versa. (Adapted from http://whatis.techtarget.com/definition/quantumtheory)

Would you rate your comprehension high, medium, or low? If you rated it high, your understanding of, and background knowledge related to, quantum physics are well above mine! If quantum physics is a topic you're not familiar with (and most of us aren't), you experienced what many EL struggling readers do when trying to navigate on-grade text. Despite reaching the end of each sentence and knowing you had decoded most words correctly, you gathered or inferred little meaning from what you read. Perhaps you went back and reread. Even then, conveying the key ideas in your own words would be difficult. For ELs, this task can feel almost impossible.

How We Monitor Comprehension

Reading is controlled by the reader. When we build meaning from text, we *comprehend.* When struggling readers do not understand what they are reading, the sense of control over their reading is lost, as well as the interest and willingness to persist in building understanding. We must help students recognize when they don't understand and teach them active strategies that can then help them do so (Palincsar and Brown 1984).

We monitor comprehension through cognitive actions that help us judge whether comprehension is taking place and decide whether and how to compensate (fix-up) (Cassanave 1988). A common indication that we don't understand is the realization that an expected idea is not confirmed or that too many concepts are unfamiliar (Palincsar and Brown 1984). When I read the previous excerpt, the concepts of *radiation from a glowing body, changing colors with rising temperature, energy existing in individual units,* and *electromagnetic waves* were all unfamiliar— unfamiliar enough that keeping up with the ideas was very difficult. Knowing little about these central ideas immediately put me off, making me stop, reread, take stock, and use strategies to try to understand. When there was still much I wasn't getting, I knew I would need to look up unfamiliar terms and read more about the related ideas. I was monitoring my comprehension.

Comprehension monitoring requires *metacognition*—being aware of how and what we're thinking. Do we progressively build understanding as we move from sentence to sentence and paragraph to paragraph, or are we distracted, confused, upset, disengaged? Once we're aware of this, we decide whether to continue reading or pause and use one or more strategies to "fix up" our understanding (Pressley and Harris 2006).

How English Proficiency Plays Out in Comprehension

For most students, informational text is more challenging than narrative text, and struggling readers and students with reading disabilities have more difficulties with it than their peers (Saenz and Fuchs 2002). Under the Common Core standards, all students are expected to read informational texts starting in kindergarten or first grade regardless of their English proficiency. By the time students reach high school, the majority of instructional time is spent reading informational text (Barton 1997). We need to mirror this focus in our instruction.

ELs face a range of issues. They may struggle with sentence complexity, length, or syntax. They may stumble over vocabulary, both general and content specific. Confusion about general terms, such as the pronouns *them* and *it,* can cause them to lose track of the main idea. Or, lacking background knowledge of content-specific terms, such as *global warming* or *filibuster*, can significantly hinder their understanding of key ideas in a text or in unit! Usually these things in combination trip them up.

No matter what difficulties readers encounter in a text, the initial remedial action is awareness. The most proficient readers are the most efficient at monitoring their comprehension. They are actively involved, have an ongoing dialogue with text (an internal think-aloud), can predict, can relate new topics to background knowledge, are able to read with a purpose, and can use appropriate fix-up strategies when needed (McKeown and Gentilucci 2007). ELs who struggle with reading monitor their comprehension less frequently than on-grade and more successful readers (Jimenez, Garcia, and Pearson 1996). Also, metacognition develops over time; although it's true that the more time students spend reading the better they become at monitoring comprehension, they also get better at it as they grow older (Baker 1985).

One Size Doesn't Fit All

Research is nuanced and should inform, but not dictate, our thinking. Not all strategies are equally useful for all ELs. Just because ELs speak another language at home does not mean they are similar in all other ways. They have varied levels of English proficiency. We need to introduce strategies when they can help, not hinder, reading. At the same time, we can't delay introducing a useful strategy too long; students need practice in order to benefit from it. Having a good sense of an EL's English proficiency helps determine when to teach a specific strategy. To activate their background knowledge, for example, students need enough English proficiency to express their thoughts. To be metacognitively aware, students need to (1) understand the steps involved, and (2) be able to articulate misunderstandings and fix them. This does not preclude teaching monitoring in the early grades. We want early readers who read *I went to the bake* instead of *I went to the bank* to be aware that the former sentence does not make sense and be able to repair it. Yet, important considerations are whether students are ready to implement the steps in comprehension monitoring and whether they have the English proficiency to understand what these steps require.

Here's something else to keep in mind: even though older, more proficient readers tend to be more aware of their comprehension struggles, researchers have found that both adults and children often overestimate how well they have understood and will retain new information (Baker and Anderson 1982; Glenberg and Epstein 1987). Based on cognitive research evidence, the case for explicit instruction on how to monitor comprehension is clear. Being aware of how easily and how often *all* readers lose the thread of comprehension calls for greater vigilance in monitoring comprehension.

There are four primary research-based approaches for helping struggling readers monitor their comprehension: (1) reciprocal teaching, (2) QRACing the code, (3) collaborative strategic reading, and (4) using G.A.U.G.E.ing, which can be tricky, so I'll highlight the particular emphases of each approach in the following sections. All four approaches frame monitoring comprehension as a problem-solving strategy (not just identifying confusion, but also resolving it) within a social context (communicating with teacher and peers). Although not all four approaches were specifically developed for ELs, they all have concrete advantages for these learners. Over time, and with enough instruction and opportunities for independent practice, EL struggling readers learn which approaches are the most useful in specific contexts.

Reciprocal Teaching

In this approach, developed three decades ago by Palincsar and Brown (1984) and initially tested with seventh-grade struggling and on-grade readers, teacher and student take turns leading a dialogue centered on relevant text features. Its value in large part is the explicit link with the purpose of reading:

> Practiced readers proceed very differently when they are reading for pleasure or to obtain a quick impression of the gist than when they are attempting to overcome a comprehension failure (debugging state) or when they are reading to meet strict criteria of understanding or retention (studying). In the first state, they read rapidly and, seemingly, effortlessly; but in the latter state, they proceed slowly and laboriously, calling into play a whole variety of learning and monitoring activities. (119)

Students learn the systematic use of four concrete strategies: (1) summarizing, (2) questioning, (3) clarifying, and (4) predicting. Figure 7–1 gives an overview of

Figure 7–1. The Four Strategies of Reciprocal Teaching

Summarizing

Teacher Prompt: *A summary is a shortened version of what you read; it doesn't include detail.*

The Power of This Strategy: *Directs students' attention to specific content and lets you check whether they've understood it. If they cannot adequately summarize what they are reading, comprehension is not proceeding as it should.*

Five Rules of Summarizing:

1. *Delete* trivia.
2. *Delete* redundancy.
3. *Superordinate* by creating a hierarchy of most important through least important information.
4. *Select* a topic sentence.
5. *Invent* a topic sentence for a paragraph where one is not explicitly stated.

Questioning

Teacher Prompt: *What question do you think someone might ask about this paragraph? If you have a hard time thinking of one, summarize first.*

The Power of This Strategy: *Focuses students' attention on main ideas and relevant supporting details and lets you monitor their understanding.*

Clarifying

Teacher Prompts: *What other words could we use in place of _____?*

What does this sentence mean?

The Power of This Strategy: *Paraphrasing helps students evaluate whether something makes sense. Putting the idea or concept into their own words lets them own it.*

Predicting

Teacher Prompts: *What might the title tell us about the article, story, or text?*

What do you think will happen next?

The Power of This Strategy: *Making predictions about future content based on recently read information helps students make and test inferences. Revisiting information while reading is key.*

Adapted from Palincsar and Brown 1984.

each. The four strategies are not always used in a specific order but, instead, in the sequence that feels most appropriate to the challenge of a specific text.

While these strategies may be familiar, the way they are used as part of reciprocal teaching may not be. Central to reciprocal teaching is the role of the teacher modeling the strategy for individual, or small groups of, students. Students then use the strategy with peers, talking about the strategy in addition to practicing it. Talking about a task deepens one's awareness of it, which is especially important for ELs because then more "academic" talk takes place. Most of the research on reciprocal teaching has been with informational text, and this research consistently shows that struggling readers are developing greater confidence with strategy use and increased comprehension (e.g., Gersten, Fuchs, Williams, and Baker 2001; Palincsar and Brown 1984; Rosenshine, Meister, and Chapman 1996). In addition to receiving individual teacher instruction and support from their peers, struggling reader ELs can be paired with more advanced EL readers or native English on-grade readers. Effective models of monitoring comprehension by a more advanced reader—whether this is the teacher or a peer who can provide clarifying language in the struggling reader's native language—are extremely helpful.

QRACing the Code

QRACing the code (Berkeley and Riccomini 2013) was initially a social studies strategy for sixth and seventh graders. The majority of both on-grade and struggling readers who were taught to QRAC the code had better recall and understanding of the material than students who took notes on three important points made in the text. ELs find it manageable and efficient. It relies mostly on student-generated questions based on chapter titles and headings. The four steps are shown in Figure 7–2.

Figure 7–2. Be a DUCKtective and QRAC the Code!

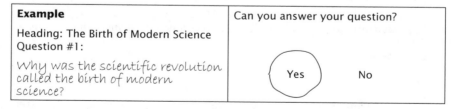

Be a DUCKtective and QRAC the Code!

Question. (Turn headings into questions.)
Read. (Read the section and STOP.)
Answer. (Ask yourself: Can I answer my question?)
Check. (Check to be sure your answer was correct or summarize the section.)

Example	Can you answer your question?
Heading: The Birth of Modern Science Question #1: *Why was the scientific revolution called the birth of modern science?*	Yes No

Need More Clues?

- Did you understand the vocabulary? ***Look for the definition of bold words.***
- Were there clues in the text features? ***Study maps and graphs.***
- Do you know anything else about the topic? ***Use your prior knowledge.***
- Was your question not answered? ***Try to summarize the section instead!***
  - » Who was the section about?
  - » Tell about the section in one or two sentences.
- Really, really stuck? ***Reread the section and try again!***

Source: Berkeley and Riccomini (2013).

The questions in QRACing the code are not leveled. This approach encourages students to say whether they can or cannot answer their question. If they can, they circle *yes* on a template listing the strategy steps. If they cannot, they circle *no* and try more fix-up strategies before continuing to the next section.

Another feature helpful for ELs is that little writing is required. Students can focus on their comprehension and not be distracted by the mechanics of composition and spelling. QRACing the code follows the guided release of responsibility (Pearson and Gallagher 1983): the teacher first explains and models, and then students have opportunities for guided and independent practice. When choosing short texts to model and practice with, it's best to use a section or page with clearly stated main ideas directly related to the section heading. This way, students get used to the strategy before applying it with more complex texts.

Collaborative Strategic Reading (CSR)

Klingner and her colleagues developed collaborative strategic reading (CSR) specifically for struggling readers (Klingner and Vaughn 1999). CSR has been used with diverse learners in grades 4 through 8, including large numbers of ELs, for more than fifteen years, mostly in the domain of social studies, and it has been proven to foster considerable growth in reading comprehension (Klingner, Vaughn, and Schumm 1998; Klingner, Vaughn, Arguelles, Hughes, and Ahwee Leftwich 2004). CSR includes explicit instruction, scaffolding, and peer discussion, as well as support for struggling readers and ELs. After modeling and explicit instruction, students, in mixed ability groups, apply four key strategies (see Figure 7–3) to text.

Figure 7–3. CSR's Four Key Strategies

- **Previewing:**
Prior to reading, students set a purpose, activate background knowledge and connect it to the text, and then predict what they will learn. Teachers have the opportunity to build knowledge through tools such as videos or graphic organizers.

- **Click and Clunk:**
Students read for meaning (*click*) and monitor their comprehension. When they notice their understanding break down (*clunk*), they use one or more of the following fix-up strategies:
  - Reread the sentence containing the clunk (the part/word you did not understand).
  - Reread sentences before and after the clunk.
  - Look for prefixes, suffixes, and root words.
  - Look for cognates.

- **Get the Gist:**
Students find the main idea—the most important *who* or *what*—in a section they have just read.

- **Wrap-Up:**
After reading, students identify the most important information in a passage. During *wrap-up* students learn how to ask literal and inferential types of questions and summarize information.

Source: Klingner et al. 1999; 2004.

The descriptive language for the CSR strategies is very student friendly and easy to remember. In particular, *Click and Clunk* is a short, applicable approach to comprehension monitoring that many struggling readers may find useful. (A collection of additional useful free resources can be found at www.toolkit.csr colorado.org.)

Using G.A.U.G.E. to Help Students Monitor Comprehension

Like QRAC-the-code and CSR, G.A.U.G.E. combines a number of strategies to help students monitor their understanding of informational text. This process was repeatedly found effective for English native speakers *and* ELs of Hispanic background in sixth and seventh grades (Richey Nuland, Taboada Barber, Whiting, and Groundwater 2014; Taboada Barber and Gallagher 2015). Developed by former social studies and ELA teachers Leila R. Nuland and Erin Ramirez, G.A.U.G.E. stands for a five-part process that includes the following steps and tools:

1. Graphically organize your understanding.
2. Ask questions.
3. Use text features or context clues.
4. Go back and reread.
5. Explain what you read.

With G.A.U.G.E., the portions of text assigned to students are longer than those in QRAC-the-code. Initial understandings are captured in graphic organizers, and text-based questions are not limited to section headings. The strategies in G.A.U.G.E. need not be followed in order; they can be combined in any number of ways. This flexibility means that students need to be comfortable using each individual strategy. We need to teach the elements of G.A.U.G.E. independently and model how to use context clues (Gunning 2014) and signal words to determine word meanings. When students are ready to read longer passages and have clear strategies for dealing with difficult vocabulary, G.A.U.G.E. is a very helpful tool.

Gradually Releasing Responsibility to Monitor Comprehension

No matter which approach to monitoring comprehension we decide is best for our students and our purpose, it's important to use the gradual release of responsibility instructional model. In the example that follows, teacher Beth Green uses G.A.U.G.E. to teach seventh graders to monitor their comprehension.

First, she has them define monitoring comprehension and consider its purpose. She writes the word *monitor* on the board, telling her students that words can have more than one meaning and that a computer monitor is not the word she wants them to consider. Then she says, "I want you, in pairs or trios, to brainstorm meanings of the word *monitor*. Specifically, think about what it means to monitor your understanding while reading." They come up with the following terms:

keep track of
check
keep watch over
control
oversee
supervise

Beth then asks, "What do you do when you monitor your reading?" During a lively discussion, the class comes up with the following definition: "Comprehension monitoring is the ability of a reader to be aware, while reading, whether a text is making sense or not." Beth then gives an example of how she monitors her reading when struggling with difficult informational text, mentioning the barriers, or stumbling blocks, listed in Figure 7–4. These barriers are especially challenging for ELs.

Next, Beth reveals a poster and bookmark (Figure 7–5) listing the G.A.U.G.E. strategies. Most of the students have already been introduced to these strategies, and they discuss how they will combine them when reading particular kinds of texts.

Figure 7–4. Barriers When Reading Informational Texts

- There are few graphic cues (although science books include more such cues than social studies books do).
- There is a less predictable sequence of ideas compared with narratives.
- The text assumes readers have the background knowledge necessary to understand the topic.
- Readers' prior knowledge may be mismatched and can interfere with comprehension.
- Topic-related vocabulary is highly technical or specific.
- General vocabulary (e.g., synthesize, establish, contribute) is also challenging and not explicitly defined.
- Text structures (e.g., cause/effect, time line/sequence, compare/contrast) vary significantly from text to text, topic to topic, and across domains (e.g., time lines are used frequently in history texts, not so much in science texts).

Figure 7–5. G.A.U.G.E. Bookmark

Graphically organize your understanding

- To show the important points of what you read.
- To connect main ideas to supporting details.
- To show meanings of new words.

Ask questions

- To help you understand what you read; ask, *Does this make sense?*
- To make you and others think more deeply.

Use text features and/or context clues

- To activate your background knowledge.
- To help you understand new vocabulary.

Go back and reread

- To help you find the main idea.
- To answer a question.
- To help you when you lose track of what you are reading.

Explain what you read

- To someone else.
- In a poster or other project.

Ask someone for help if you still don't understand!

Now Beth thinks aloud as she demonstrates the main steps in monitoring comprehension:

1. She stumbles over the meaning of a paragraph she's reading.
2. She picks a G.A.U.G.E. strategy to help her.
3. She applies the strategies in G.A.U.G.E. to improve her comprehension.
4. She chooses and applies additional strategies until her comprehension is thorough and solid.

As she models, she points to context clues for difficult words (Figure 7–6) and signal words (Figure 7–7) that help her understand what she's reading. Of course, these clues and words will vary depending on the comprehension challenge—word meaning, sentence complexity, and limited background knowledge—that a text presents.

Because G.A.U.G.E. is a combination of several strategies and tools, Beth gives her students ample time to practice them and provides scaffolding as they do. Initially they try these strategies for only ten minutes at a time and use sticky notes to record their thinking as they encounter difficulties and try to address them.

After her students have had time to apply G.A.U.G.E., Beth asks them to capture important information, connections, and questions on a graphic organizer (see Figure 7–8). They then use this information as the basis for discussions of the texts they have read and the strategies they used when they stumbled over meaning.

Figure 7–6. Context Clues for Difficult Words

Definition: *A crutch is a metal or wooden stick that fits under the armpit to help people walk when they have a foot or leg injury.*

Synonym: *The periphery, or border, of that country is _____ .*

Comparison/Contrast: *The weather was bad; <u>however</u>, we still went outside.*

Function Indicator: *The chassis ovens, as well as the cab ovens, are heated with the help of the plant incinerator.* (What does an *incinerator* do?)

Example: *Some animals have a mostly carnivorous diet; they eat other animals and do not eat many plants.*

Pictorial Clue: *A visual representation of the word's meaning.*

Adapted from Gunning 2014.

Figure 7–7. Signal Words to Pay Attention to When Monitoring Comprehension

is/are, was/were, means, or, such as, known as, called, as well as

(used with definitions, synonyms, examples, function indicators)

not, but, however, even though

(used with compare and contrast statements)

Examples of Signal Words:

Definition:	Mark Twain **is** a <u>pseudonym</u>. A <u>pseudonym</u> **is** a fake name.
	Triangles that are the same shape and size **are known as** <u>congruent</u>.
	Animals that are cold-blooded, lay eggs, have scales, and breathe with lungs **are called** <u>reptiles</u>.
Explanation:	A unicorn **is** a <u>mythological</u> animal. <u>Mythological</u> **means** made up.
Synonym/Definition:	<u>Glaciers</u>, **or** slowly moving rivers of ice, formed over many parts of the Earth.
Example:	I like to eat green <u>vegetables</u> **such as** broccoli and green beans.
Contrast:	I know green <u>vegetables</u> are good for you, **even though** I do not like all of them.
	Reptiles are cold-blooded so they can adapt their bodies easily to the environment; **however,** scientists do not like the term cold-blooded, because it is imprecise.

Figure 7–8. Graphic Organizer to Use with G.A.U.G.E.

Name _____ Number _____ Topic _____

Important Information	Connections: to self, to text, to world	My Questions

Collaboration as a Scaffold for Monitoring Comprehension

The purpose of student collaboration as a support for reading motivation is that, together, students will learn more. True student collaboration takes place when students need to talk with one another to complete a task. Most students enjoy working together (Johnson and Johnson 1985), so they are likely to become more engaged in a task when they are able to put their heads together and exchange ideas. Research shows that collaborative activities promote oral second language learning when ELs interact with both native speakers and other ELs (Gass 2003; Gass and Mackey 2007; Long 1996; Pica 1994). Collaborative activities are also key to successful and engaged reading comprehension. Both reciprocal teaching and collaborative strategic reading rely heavily on student collaboration.

The challenge with having students monitor their comprehension independently is providing enough structure so struggling readers don't lose sight of the main goal, which is to build meaning from text. Given the many facets involved, EL struggling readers may feel overwhelmed by the process, so it's essential to provide continued modeling with plenty of opportunities for guided and collaborative practice.

One way to do this is through partner reading, because taking turns reading, both aloud and silently, with a partner keeps students engaged in the process. I recommend pairing ELs with on-grade or above-grade native English speakers. However, the gap in reading and language ability should not be so broad that the stronger reader dominates the interaction.

A challenge in implementing student collaboration successfully, especially with ELs, is the inequity inherent in the classroom social system. Students seen as high achievers or socially popular tend to dominate the dynamics of the group, while lower-status students tend to be less listened to or included in group decisions (National Academies Press 2004). Often, ELs fall within the latter group. Therefore, we need to think and plan in advance how to facilitate *meaningful* student collaboration in which ELs benefit as much from shared literacy tasks as their native-English-speaking peers who do not struggle with reading.

Another way to foster meaningful student collaboration is through small guided-reading groups. Students read and apply strategies on their own, but then discuss the text and their use of strategies in small groups. To counteract negative group dynamics, we need to provide explicit criteria for successful collaboration, as described in Figure 7–9.

Figure 7–9. Criteria for Successful Small-Group Collaboration in Literacy Tasks

1. It is necessary for students to talk with one another to accomplish the task.
2. A question or problem is central to the task. (This stimulates students to collaborate as they formulate, share, and compare ideas.)
3. The task at hand is broad enough to ensure both individual and group accountability (Vaca, Lapp, and Fisher 2011).
4. A number of rotating student roles are encouraged.
5. ELs are given sufficient opportunities to express themselves as group members.
6. Both individual and group ideas are reported and shared with the class.
7. The literacy task is one in which students' responses can vary.
8. Texts of varying lengths, topics, and levels are provided, so students of different reading levels feel equally challenged.
9. Group behavioral rules are set in advance.
10. More than one way to respond to the task is provided (e.g., various kinds of student charts, graphic organizers, ways of reporting) so that all students can show their contributions to the group's effort.

Many middle school ELs are enthusiastic about and appreciate the benefits of effective collaboration. When I asked seventh-grader Anastasia how she felt about collaboration as part of USHER, she said:

> I liked that we could ask questions to each other in pairs. We listened to the questions and really tried to answer them. Sometimes we ask the questions with the whole class, but I do not always listen or understand them. Here it was more private—"you ask, I listen, we read"—and then we tried to come up with answers together. That was fun! I felt I had to pay attention to my reading when doing that.

We can increase the positive effects of peer collaboration by letting students choose what to read within these partner and group pairings. Research with middle school struggling readers (Ivey and Johnston 2013), both native English speakers and ELs, has shown that when adolescents are given opportunities to select personally meaningful young adult books and time to read them, they read for longer periods. Allowing students to choose their own books also generates spontaneous conversations among students who have read the same book, as well as book recommendations. Shared knowledge about books can also ease social tension ("it's like an ice breaker"). Students make new friendships and deepen existing ones through shared reading experiences. Although this study did not include informational books, it offers strong evidence that meaningful literature choices encourage student collaboration. Thus, there appears to be a reciprocal relationship between engagement and collaborative literacy activities. Students read more as a result of collaborating with others on reading tasks, and this deep, extended, focused reading leads to meaningful collaborative outcomes.

Complex to Teach, But Essential to Learn

Despite the apparent complexity, all students, ELs in particular, need to be taught to monitor their comprehension. Many ELs see their struggle to read as a failing rather than a process, and monitoring comprehension communicates that reading is a process (Block 1992). Strong, mature readers do not expect to understand everything they read. They are ready to monitor their understanding and question what they do and don't understand. ELs need to be made aware that questioning and monitoring confusion is a part of good reading, not the result of an imperfect knowledge of English (Block 1992; Taboada, Kidd and Tonks 2010).

All students, not just ELs, will improve their comprehension if they are taught to identify the source of their difficulty. A major difference between more- and less-proficient EL readers is their awareness of the source of the problems they encounter (Block 1992; Jimenez 1997). This awareness is a necessary preliminary step to fixing any misunderstanding; it may be just as important as knowing the appropriate tool or fix-up strategy to deal with the misunderstanding (Block 1992). Teaching ELs that comprehension challenges can be attributed to a source or cause rather than to lack of skill is an important part of effective reading instruction that builds students' self-efficacy (Taboada Barber and Gallagher 2015), and promotes knowledge goals—or learning for the sake of learning—all important dimensions of engaged reading.

When the *EL* Label No Longer Feels Like a Barrier

As we help our ELs read and understand informational text, we need to keep in mind that although we use the term *English Learner,* ELs are learning English while at the same time learning all the other content our non-ELs need to learn. Our instruction may sometimes, consciously or not, focus on one at the expense of the other, because we know what a heavy load learning both language and content can be. But that doesn't mean we need to lower expectations. ELs can carry that identity around for a long time; they may feel like English Learners well into their adult lives. They may be proud of speaking another language, or they may not. In either case, engaged reading is even more necessary for struggling reader ELs than it is for avid native English readers. Precisely because their academic load can be heavy, ELs need motivational supports to read. We can honor the fact that it takes time to become proficient in English while also working diligently to guide ELs toward engaged, proficient reading.

Fostering Lasting Change

Not long ago I received an email from Sandra, a tenth grader who had participated in a research project I had led four years earlier. She wanted to tell me that *her life had been changed* (her words) by *The Orphan of Ellis Island,* by Elvira Woodruff, which we had read as the launching narrative for a social studies unit on immigration. She explained that the book helped her understand that "coming to a new country to live is like being adopted by a family. When I finished the book I understood those were similar things." Propelled by this realization, Sandra kept reading. She asked her teacher for resources and then visited her school and local libraries, acquiring new knowledge about the experience of immigration from a number of other books: *Coming to America: The Story of Immigration,* by Betsy Maestro and Susannah Ryan; *If Your Name Was Changed at Ellis Island,* by Ellen Levine and Wayne Parmenter; *Immigrant Kids,* by Russell Freedman; and *Immigration,* by Peter Benoit. Clearly, she read extensively about immigration, well beyond school-related requirements and standards.

But Sandra's reason for reaching out to me went beyond sharing a list of books. She realized that *she had been changed by and through reading*. Through these texts she had come to better understand herself and her family's journey from El Salvador to the United States. I wrote this book in the belief that we can help all EL readers become like Sandra: an engaged, self-identified voracious reader who is thriving academically. Sandra's email also made me wonder more about her journey. What were the pivotal points besides Woodruff's book for her success? How can we create the same kind of success for other EL readers?

Fostering a positive reading identity and the ability to read informational texts successfully requires more than a unit on immigration (although that's a worthy topic). To do this work, we have to provide *daily* doses of explicit instruction on comprehension strategies, an appealing variety of informational texts, and motivational support.

The belief that our teaching can influence student reading engagement motivates our instruction throughout the academic year. It helps to remind ourselves of the kind of growth that's possible for our EL readers. At the beginning of sixth grade, Sandra had been a shy, quiet student who struggled with reading. Lacking confidence in her English ability, she avoided almost every academic conversation. Although she had been in the United States three years, she was reading at the third-grade level and exhibited an emerging level of English proficiency. With good intentions but little understanding, her teachers had been doing her work for her: telling her what words meant, reading paragraphs aloud and then telling her what the main ideas were, writing down answers that reflected their thinking more than hers. They wanted her to learn how to read but never gave her a positive reason to engage. Despite the large number of Spanish-speaking ELs in her school, Sandra saw ELs who struggled academically being pulled out of the regular science and social studies classes and into the resource room. Making that trip a couple of times herself, she realized this was not fun and she didn't learn much there. But back in her classroom, where English was spoken all day at a fast space, she was anxious, and her anxiety only increased when she had to share or discuss her textbook reading. In writing and in conversation, she was asked lots of teacher-generated questions meant mostly to assess comprehension. Little was done to invite her to explore ideas or expand her understanding and no space was created for self-directed work.

Boring instruction is often poor instruction. Content-area reading instruction devoid of motivation may fulfill test requirements but will not empower our ELs to learn from informational texts on their own. As teachers, we can't just resign ourselves to the idea that informational texts are boring, required "medicine" for school. We communicate something much larger than genre preference when we do. We actively disinvite our students from one of the essential reasons to read: to learn more about the world. For many of our ELs, the typical textbook-only informational reading they are given in school communicates that they won't be learning from reading. How can that not translate into thinking they won't learn in school, period?

The good news shared in this book is that with our support ELs can become motivated, engaged readers who read to learn. Part of that support comes from the cognitive tools we provide to harness our students' reading experiences. Another part comes from classroom structure, the motivational practices we instill to hook them into reading. When we make motivation part of reading instruction, we show ELs that education is about identity and agency: we acknowledge who they are right now and invite them to grow through and by reading.

This growth will only happen if we motivate students and help them experience joy and curiosity in their own reading. I hope this book has reinforced the idea that student engagement can be deepened by purposefully teaching motivational practices together with comprehension strategies. As ELs become more confident learners through the daily practices we undertake with them, they will discover the pleasure of reading, which will then fire their motivation. This will also help us build a community of learners who share some of the same challenges, regardless of their first language.

To accomplish this, it is vital that ELs not see their language background as a barrier. Our job in teaching how to learn from informational texts includes underscoring this message and reminding ELs that *all* students struggle with the challenges in informational texts, throughout their education. The comprehension strategies and motivational practices discussed in this book help us and our students identify tools to use with informational texts that foster curiosity rather than frustration.

We can't predict when students will shift from disengaged to engaged or how long it will take, but we can provide opportunities that ensure they do. Fourth-grader Marina's engagement with informational texts came when she was shown how to set her own content-learning goals "beyond doing better than my classmates." Seventh-grader Marisa started down the path of real growth as a reader when she got to choose her expert topic. Thomas became a different kind of reader in eighth grade when he was given the opportunity to display knowledge from a text in a creative, unusual way. For an EL reader in your classroom, it may be discovering the importance of reading about the Articles of the Confederation or the solar system or being given opportunities to collaborate. We can't predict, so we provide opportunity.

Strategic Tools and Motivational Practices

You now have some strategies and practices to provide purposeful, scaffolded academic opportunities for your EL readers, opportunities for them to build their cognitive skills while also deepening their engagement in their own learning. It's up to you to choose how and when you'll incorporate these tools. The pairings of motivational practices with reading strategies provided in this book are only models: your combinations will almost certainly be different. That's wonderful. The point is to make sure that reading strategy instruction is always explicit, includes the gradual release of responsibility, and features at least one motivational practice. There are many ways you can make this happen in your classroom.

Final Thoughts

When you finish reading this last page, what I hope remains is a sense of urgency to do this work tomorrow and a commitment to the long view—making this part of your daily instruction throughout the year—so that all EL readers in your classroom have the opportunity to become stronger readers, to learn more through their reading, to see themselves as engaged lifelong learners. We have that power—and responsibility—as teachers.

References

Alderman, M. K. 2008. *Motivation for Achievement: Possibilities for Teaching and Learning*, 3rd ed. New York: Routledge.

Alvermann, D. 2001. *Effective Literacy Instruction for Adolescents*. Executive Summary and Paper commissioned by the National Reading Conference. Chicago: National Reading Conference.

Ames, C. 1992. "Classrooms: Goals, Structures, and Student Motivation." *Journal of Educational Psychology* 84 (3): 261–271. doi:10.1037/0022-0663.84.3.261.

Anderman, E., M. L. Maehr, and C. Midgley. 1999. "Declining Motivation After the Transition to Middle School: Schools Can Make a Difference." *Journal of Research and Development in Education* 32: 131–147.

Anderson, R. C. 1978. "Schema-Directed Processes in Language Comprehension." In *Cognitive Psychology and Instruction*, edited by A. Lesgold, J. Pellegrino, S. Fokkema, and R. Glaser. New York: Plenum.

Anderson, R. C., and P. Freebody. 1981. "Vocabulary Knowledge." In *Comprehension and Teaching: Research Reviews*, edited by J. Guthrie, 77–117. Newark, DE: International Reading Association.

Anderson, R. C., and P. D. Pearson. 1984. "A Schema-Theoretic View of Basic Processes in Reading. In *Handbook of Reading Research,* edited by P. Pearson, 255–291. New York: Longman.

Anderson, R., J. Pichert, and L. Shirey. 1983. "Effects of the Reader's Schema at Different Points in Time." *Journal of Educational Psychology* 75: 271–279.

Anglin, J. M. 1993. "Vocabulary Development: A Morphological Analysis." *Monographs of the Society for Research in Child Development* 58 (10).

Ash, G. E. 2002. "Teaching Readers Who Struggle: A Pragmatic Middle School Framework." *Reading Online* 5 (7). Retrieved from www.readingonline.org/articles /art_index.asp?HREF = ash/index.html.

Assor, A., H. Kaplan, and G. Roth. 2002. "Choice Is Good, but Relevance Is Excellent: Autonomy-Enhancing and Suppressing Teacher Behaviours Predicting Students' Engagement in Schoolwork." *British Journal of Educational Psychology* 72 (2): 261–278. doi:10.1348/000709902158883.

August, D., and K. Hakuta, eds. 1997. *Improving Schooling for Language-Minority Children: A Research Agenda.* Washington, DC: National Academy Press.

August, D., L. Shanahan, and T. Shanahan. 2006. *Developing Literacy in Second-Language Learners: Lessons from the Report of the National Literacy Panel on Language Minority Children and Youth.* New York: Routledge.

Avalos, M. A., A. Plasencia, C. Chavez, and J. Rascón. 2007. "Modified Guided Reading: Gateway to English as a Second Language and Literacy Learning." *The Reading Teacher* 61 (4): 318–329. doi:10.1598/RT.61.4.4.

Baker, D. L., Y. Park, S. K. Baker, D. Basaraba, E. Kame'enui, and C. Thomas Beck. 2012. "Effects of a Paired Bilingual Reading Program on the Reading Performance of English Learners in Grades 1–3." *Journal of School Psychology* 50 (6): 737–58. doi:10.1016/j.jsp.2012.09.002.

Baker, L. 1985. "Differences in the Standards Used by College Students to Evaluate Their Comprehension of Expository Prose." *Reading Research Quarterly* 20: 297–313.

Baker, L., and R. I. Anderson. 1982. "Effects of Inconsistent Information on Text Processing: Evidence for Comprehension Monitoring." *Reading Research Quarterly* 17: 281–294.

Baker, L., and W. Saul. 1994. "Considering Science and Language Arts Connections: A Study of Teacher Cognition." *Journal of Research in Science Teaching* 31 (9): 1023–1037.

Baker, L., and A. Wigfield. 1999. "Dimensions of Children's Motivation for Reading and Their Relation to Reading Activity and Achievement." *Reading Research Quarterly* 34: 452–477.

Baker, S., N. Lesaux, M. Jayanthi, J. Dimino, C. P. Proctor, J. Morris, R. Gersten, K. Haymond, M. J. Kieffer, S. Linan-Thompson, and R. Newman-Gonchar. 2014. *Teaching Academic Content and Literacy to English Learners in Elementary and Middle School* (NCEE 2014-4012). Washington, DC: National Center for Education Evaluation and Regional Assistance (NCEE), Institute of Education Sciences, U.S. Department of Education. Retrieved from the NCEE website: http://ies.ed.gov/ncee/wwc/publications_reviews.aspx.

Bandura, A. 1997. *Self-Efficacy: The Exercise of Control.* New York: W. H. Freeman.

Barton, M. L. 1997. "Addressing the Literacy Crisis: Teaching Reading in the Content Areas." *National Association of Secondary School Principals* 81: 22–30.

Baumann, J. F. 1982. "Children's Ability to Comprehend Main Ideas After Reading Expository Prose." Paper presented at the annual meeting of the National Reading Conference, Dallas, TX, December 2–5, 1981. ERIC Document Reproduction Service No. ED 211945.

———. 1983. "Teaching Children to Comprehend Main Ideas." Paper presented at the annual meeting of the National Reading Conference, Clearwater Beach, FL, December 4–6, 1982. ERIC Document Reproduction Service No. ED228623.

Baumann, J. F. E., C. Edwards, G. Font, C. A. Tereshinski., E. J. Kame'enui, and S. Olejnik. 2002. "Teaching Morphemic and Contextual Analysis to Fifth-Grade Students." *Reading Research Quarterly* 37 (2): 150–176. doi:10.1598/RRQ.37.2.3.

Bear, D. R., M. Invernizzi, S. Templeton, and F. Johnston. 2012. *Words Their Way: Word Study for Phonics, Vocabulary, and Spelling Instruction*, 5th ed. Upper Saddle River, NJ: Pearson Prentice-Hall.

Beck, I. L., M. G. McKeown, and L. Kucan. 2002. *Bringing Words to Life: Robust Vocabulary Instruction*. New York: Guilford.

———. 2013. *Bringing Words to Life: Robust Vocabulary Instruction,* 2nd ed. New York: Guilford.

Beck, J. S., A. Taboada Barber, and M. M. Buehl. 2013. "It's Just Something About the Past: Students' Perceptions of Reading and Learning in Social Studies." Paper presented at the 63rd annual Literacy Research Association Conference, Dallas, TX, December 4.

Benware, C. A., and E. L. Deci. 1984. "Quality of Learning with an Active Versus Passive Motivational Set." *American Educational Research Journal* 21 (4): 755–765.

Berkeley, S., and P. J. Riccomini. 2013. "QRAC-the-Code: A Comprehension Monitoring Strategy for Middle School Social Studies Textbooks." *Journal of Learning Disabilities* 46: 154–165.

Bialystok, E., G. Luk, and E. Kwan. 2005. "Bilingualism, Biliteracy, and Learning to Read: Interactions Among Languages and Writing Systems." *Scientific Studies of Reading* 9 (1): 43–61. doi:10.1207/s1532799xssr0901_4.

Biancarosa, G., and C. Snow. 2006. *Reading Next—A Vision for Action and Research in Middle and High School Literacy: A Report to Carnegie Corporation of New York.* Washington, DC: Alliance for Excellent Education.

Blachowicz, C. L. Z., and P. J. Fisher. 2007. *Best Practices in Vocabulary Instruction.* In *Best Practices in Literacy Instruction,* edited by L. B. Gambrell, M. Morrow, and M. Pressley, 178–203. New York: Guilford.

Black, A. E., and E. L. Deci. 2000. "The Effects of Instructors' Autonomy Support and Students' Autonomous Motivation on Learning Organic Chemistry: A Self-Determination Theory Perspective." *Science Education* 84 (6): 740–756. http://doi.org/10.1002/1098-237X(200011)84:6<740::AID-SCE4>3.0.CO;2-3.

Block, E. 1992. "See How They Read: Comprehension Monitoring of L1 and L2 Readers." *TESOL Quarterly* 26 (2): 319–343.

Bransford, J. D. 2004. "Schema Activation and Schema Acquisition: Comments on Richard C. Anderson's Remarks." In *Theoretical Models and Processes of Reading*, 5th ed., edited by R. Ruddell and N. Unrau, 607–619. Newark, DE: International Reading Association.

Brophy, J. 1999. "Toward a Model of the Value Aspects of Motivation in Education: Developing Appreciation for Particular Learning Domains and Activities." *Educational Psychologist* 34 (2): 75–85.

Brown, C. L. 2007. "Supporting English Language Learners in Content-Reading." *Reading Improvement* 44 (1): 32–39.

Brown, R., M. Pressley, P. Van Meter, and T. Schuder. 1996. "A Quasi-Experimental Validation of Transactional Strategies Instruction with Low-Achieving Second-Grade Readers." *Journal of Educational Psychology* 88 (1): 18–37.

Bulgren, J. A., D. D. Deshler, J. B. Schumaker, and B. K. Lenz. 2000. "The Use and Effectiveness of Analogical Instruction in Diverse Secondary Content Classrooms." *Journal of Educational Psychology* 92 (3): 426–441. doi:10.1037/0022-0663.92.3.426.

Burgan, M. 2006. *A Changing Nation: Immigration and Industrialization from the Civil War to World War I*. Chicago: Heinemann Library.

Burgoyne, K., J. M. Kelly, H. E. Whiteley, and A. Spooner. 2010. "The Comprehension of Children Learning English as an Additional Language." *British Journal of Educational Psychology* 79: 735–747. doi:10.1348/000709909X422530.

Cain, K., and J. Oakhill. 2009. "Reading Comprehension Development from 8 to 14 Years: The Contribution of Component Skills and Processes." In *Beyond Decoding: The Behavioral and Biological Foundations of Reading Comprehension,* edited by R. Wagner, C. Schatschneider, and C. Phythian-Sence. New York: Guilford.

Campbell, J. R., K. E. Voelkl, and P. T. Donahue. 1997. *NAEP 1996 Trends in Academic Progress*. NCES Publication no. 97-985. Washington, DC: U.S. Department of Education.

Carlisle, J. F. 2010. "Effects of Instruction in Morphological Awareness on Literacy Achievement: An Integrative Review." *Reading Research Quarterly* 45 (4): 464–487. doi:dx.doi.org/10.1598/RRQ.45.4.5.

Carlo, M. S., D. August, B. Mclaughlin, C. E. Snow, C. Dressler, D. N. Lippman, C. E. White. 2004. "Closing the Gap: Addressing the Vocabulary Needs of English-Language Learners in Bilingual and Mainstream Classrooms." *Reading Research Quarterly* 39 (2): 188–215. doi:10.1598/RRQ.39.2.3.

Carver, R. 1994. "Percentage of Unknown Vocabulary Words in Text as a Function of the Relative Difficulty of the Text: Implications for Instruction." *Journal of Reading Behavior* 26: 413–437.

Casanave, C. P. 1988. "Comprehension Monitoring in ESL Reading: A Neglected Essential." *TESOL Quarterly* 22: 283–302.

Cervetti, G. N., J. Barber, R. Dorph, P. D. Pearson, and P. G. Goldschmidt. 2012. "The Impact of an Integrated Approach to Science and Literacy in Elementary School Classrooms." *Journal of Research in Science Teaching* 49 (5): 631–658. doi:10.1002/tea.21015.

Chang, G. L., and G. Wells. 1987. "The Literate Potential of Collaborative Talk." Paper presented at the meeting of the International Oracy Convention, Norwich, England, March 30–April 3.

Chin, C., and J. Osborne. 2010. "Supporting Argumentation Through Students' Questions: Case Studies in Science Classrooms." *Journal of the Life Sciences* 19 (2): 230–284.

Chiodo, J. J., and J. Byford. 2004. "Do They Really Dislike Social Studies? A Study of Middle School and High School Students." *Journal of Social Studies Research* 28 (1): 16–26.

Cipriano, J. 2003. *Native Americans*. Pelham, NY: Benchmark Education.

Clark, F. L., D. D. Deshler, J. B. Schumaker, G. R. Alley, and M. M. Warner. 1984. "Visual Imagery and Self-Questioning: Strategies to Improve Comprehension of Written Material." *Journal of Learning Disabilities* 17: 145–149.

Cobb, C., and C. Blachowicz. 2014. *No More "Look Up the List" Vocabulary Instruction*. Portsmouth, NH: Heinemann.

Cohen, E. G. 1994. "Restructuring the Classroom: Conditions for Productive Small Groups." *Review of Educational Research* 64 (1). doi:10.3102/00346543064001001.

Collier, V. P. 1989. "How Long? A Synthesis of Research on Academic Achievement in a Second Language." *TESOL Quarterly* 23: 509–531.

Connell, J. P. 1990. "Context, Self, and Action: A Motivational Analysis of Self-System Processes Across the Lifespan." In *The Self in Transition: Infancy to Childhood,* edited by D. Cicchetti and M. Beeghly, 61–97. Chicago: University of Chicago Press.

Cooper, J. 2003. *Life Cycle of a Monarch Butterfly*. Vero Beach, FL: Rourke.

Corbin, S. S. 1997. "Comparisons with Other Academic Subjects and Selected Influences on High School Students' Attitudes Toward Social Studies." *Journal of Social Studies Research* 21 (2): 13–18.

Cordova, D. I., and M. R. Lepper. 1996. "Intrinsic Motivation and the Process of Learning: Beneficial Effects of Contextualization, Personalization, and Choice." *Journal of Educational Psychology* 88 (4): 715–730. doi:10.1037/0022-0663.88.4.715.

Cox, K., and J. T. Guthrie. 2002. "Concept Instruction with Text." In *Literacy in America: An Encyclopedia of History, Theory, and Practice*, edited by B. Guzzetti, 90–93. New York: ABC-CLIO.

Cummins, J. 1981a. *Bilingualism and Language Minority Children*. Toronto, ON: OISE Press.

———. 1981b. "The Role of Primary Language Development in Promoting Educational Success for Language Minority Students." In *Schooling and Language Minority Students: A Theoretical Framework,* edited by California State Department of Education, 33–49. Los Angeles: National Dissemination and Assessment Center.

Cunningham, A. E., and K. E. Stanovich. 1997. "Early Reading Acquisition and Its Relation to Reading Experience and Ability 10 Years Later." *Developmental Psychology* 33: 934–945.

Cunningham, K., and P. Benoit. 2011. *The Inuit*. New York: Children's Press.

Czajka, C. W. n.d. "Uncle Sam Is Rich Enough to Give Us All a Farm: Homesteaders, the Frontier, and Hopscotching Across America." Retrieved from www.pbs.org/wnet/frontierhouse/frontierlife/essay1.html.

Davis, B. D. 1968. "Research in Comprehension in Reading." *Reading Research Quarterly* 3 (4): 499–545.

Davis-Kean, P. E. 2006. "Stimulating the Next Generation." *Wider Benefits of Learning Update* 3 (Spring): 2.

Davies, M. n.d. *Words and Phrase*. Retrieved from http://www.wordandphrase.info/.

De La Paz, S., and M. K. Felton. 2010. "Reading and Writing from Multiple Source Documents in History: Effects of Strategy Instruction with Low to Average High School Writers." *Contemporary Educational Psychology* 35 (3): 174–192. doi:10.1016/j.cedpsych.2010.03.001.

Deshler, D. D., E. S. Ellis, and B. K. Lenz. 1996. *Teaching Adolescents with Learning Disabilities: Strategies and Methods.* Denver, CO: Love Publishing.

Discovery Education (producer). n.d. *American History: At the Western Frontier* (online video). Available from http://player.discoveryeducation.com/index.cfm?guidAssetID = C8A6DB97-1E49-43CA-9FDD-D146FD52B7DA&productcode = US.

———. n.d. *Boom or Bust: Mining and the Opening of the American West* (online video). Available from http://player.discoveryeducation.com/index.cfm?guidAssetID = B544C7D0-5402-4432-8722-04427466A801&productcode = US.

———. n.d. *The Real American Cowboy* (online video). Available from http://player.discoveryeducation.com/index.cfm?guidAssetID = CEC1158B-127C-40C9-A01D-0C6670D983CA&productcode = US.

Doiron, R. 1994. "Using Nonfiction in a Read-Aloud Program: Letting the Facts Speak for Themselves." *Reading Teacher* 47 (8): 616–624.

Dole, J. A., G. G. Duffy, L. R. Roehler, and P. D. Pearson. 1991. "Moving from the Old to the New: Research on Reading Comprehension Instruction." *Review of Educational Research* 61: 239–264.

Duke, N. K. 2000. "3.6 Minutes per Day: The Scarcity of Informational Texts in First Grade." *Reading Research Quarterly* 35 (2): 202–224. doi:10.1598/RRQ.35.2.1.

———. 2004. "The Case for Informational Text." *Educational Leadership* 61 (6): 40–44. Retrieved from www.ascd.org/publications/educational_leadership.aspx.

Duke, N. K., and J. Kays. 1998. "'Can I say, "Once upon a time"?' Kindergarten Children Developing Knowledge of Information Book Language." *Early Childhood Research Quarterly* 13 (2): 295–318.

Duke, N. K, P. D. Pearson, S. L. Strachan, A. K. Billman. 2011. "Essential Elements of Fostering and Teaching Reading Comprehension." In *What Research Has to Say About Reading Instruction,* 4th ed., edited by S. Samuels and A. Farstrup, 51–93. Newark, DE: International Reading Association.

Dunn, B., S. R. Mathews, and G. Bieger. 1979. *Individual Differences in the Recall of Lower-Level Textual Information.* Tech. Rep. No. 150. Urbana-Champaign: University of Illinois, Center for the Study of Reading.

Dweck, C. S., and E. L. Leggett. 1988. "A Social-Cognitive Approach to Motivation and Personality." *Psychological Review* 95 (2): 256–273. doi:10.1037/0033-295X.95.2.256.

Eccles, J. S., and A. Wigfield. 2002. "Motivational Beliefs, Values, and Goals." *Annual Review of Psychology* 53 (1):109–132. doi:10.1146/annurev.psych.53.100901.135153.

Faggella-Luby, M., J. S. Schumaker, and D. D. Deshler. 2007. "Embedded Learning Strategy Instruction: Story-Structure Pedagogy in Heterogeneous Secondary Literature Classes." *Learning Disability Quarterly* 30 (2): 131–147.

Fernandez, C., G. C. Massey, and S. M. Dornbusch. 1975. *High School Students' Perceptions of Social Studies.* Stanford, CA: Stanford Center for Research and Development in Teaching. ERIC Document Reproduction Service No. ED113241.

Fernandez, C., G. C. Massey, and S. M. Dombusch. 1976. "High School Students' Perceptions of Social Studies." *The Social Studies* 57 (2): 51–57.

Fitzgerald, J. 1995. "English-as-a-Second-Language Reading Instruction in the United States: A Research Review." *Journal of Reading Behavior* 27 (2): 115–152.

Flanagan, A. K. 1998. *The Pueblos.* New York: Children's Press.

Fredricks, J. A., P. C. Blumenfeld, and A. H. Paris. 2004. "School Engagement: Potential of the Concept, State of the Evidence." *Review of Educational Research* 74 (1): 59–109. doi:10.3102/00346543074001059.

Frey, N., and D. Fisher. 2006. *Language Arts Workshop: Purposeful Reading and Writing Instruction.* Upper Saddle River, NJ: Merrill Education.

Gambrell, L., B. Palmer, R. Codling, and S. Mazzoni. 1996. "Assessing Motivation to Read." *The Reading Teacher* 49: 518–533.

García, E. 1999. *Student Cultural Diversity: Understanding and Meeting the Challenge,* 2nd ed. Boston: Houghton Mifflin.

Gass, S. M. 2003. "Input and Interaction." In *The Handbook of Second Language Acquisition,* edited by C. J. Doughty, and M. H. Long, 224–255. Malden, MA: Blackwell.

Gass, S. M., and A. Mackey. 2007. "Input, Interaction, and Output in Second Language Acquisition." In *Theories in Second Language Acquisition: An Introduction,* edited by B. VanPatten and J. Williams, 175–199. Mahwah, NJ: Erlbaum.

Gathercole, V. C. 2002. "Monolingual and Bilingual Acquisition: Learning Different Treatments of That-Trace Phenomena in English and Spanish." In *Language and Literacy Development in Bilingual Children,* edited by D. K. Oller and R. Eilers, 220–254. Clevedon, UK: Multilingual Matters.

George, J. C. 1972. *Julie of the Wolves.* New York: HarperTrophy.

Gersten, R., L. Fuchs, J. Williams, and S. Baker. 2001. "Teaching Reading Comprehension Strategies to Students with Learning Disabilities: A Review of Research." *Review of Educational Research* 71 (2): 279–320.

Gettinger, M., and M. J. Walter. 2012. "Classroom Strategies to Enhance Academic Engaged Time." In *Handbook of Research on Student Engagement*, edited by S. Christenson, A. L. Reschly, and C. Wylie, 653–673. New York: Springer.

Gillis, V. 2014. "Disciplinary Literacy." *Journal of Adolescent & Adult Literacy* 57 (8): 614–623. doi:10.1002/jaal.301.

Glenberg, A. M., and W. Epstein. 1985. "Calibration of Comprehension." *Journal of Experimental Psychology: Learning Memory, and Cognition* 11 (4): 702–718.

Goerss, B. L., I. L. Beck, and M. G. McKeown. 1999. "Increasing Remedial Students' Ability to Derive Word Meaning from Context." *Reading Psychology* 20 (2): 151–175. doi:10.1080/027027199278457.

Goldman, S. R., and J. A. Rakestraw. 2000. "Structural Aspects of Constructing Meaning from Text." In *Handbook of Reading Research,* vol. 3, edited by M. L. Kamil, P. B. Mosenthal, P. D. Pearson, and R. Barr, 311–335. Mahwah, NJ: Erlbaum.

Gottfried, A.W. 1985. "Measures of SocioEconomic Status in Child Development Research: Data and Recommendations." *Merrill-Palmer Quarterly* 31 (1): 85–92.

Gottfried, A. E., G. A. Marcoulides, A. W. Gottfried, P. Oliver, and D. Guerin. 2007. "Multivariate Latent Change Modeling of Developmental Decline in Academic Intrinsic Math Motivation and Achievement: Childhood Through Adolescence." *International Journal of Behavioral Development* 31: 317–327.

Gottlieb, M. 2006. *Assessing English Language Learners: Bridges from Language Proficiency to Academic Achievement*. Thousand Oaks, CA: Corwin Press.

Graham, I. 2000. *You Wouldn't Want to Work on the Railroad! A Track You'd Rather Not Go Down*. Danbury, CT: Children's Press.

Graham, S., and S. Golan. 1991. "Motivational Influences on Cognition: Task Involvement, Ego Involvement, and Depth of Information Processing." *Journal of Educational Psychology* 83 (2): 187–194.

Graves, M. F. 2000. "A Vocabulary Program to Complement and Bolster a Middle-Grade Comprehension Program." In *Reading for Meaning: Fostering Comprehension in the Middle Grades*, edited by B. M. Taylor, M. F. Graves, and P. Van den Broek, 116–135. Newark, DE: International Reading Association.

———. 2006. *The Vocabulary Book: Learning and Instruction*. New York: Teacher's College Press.

Graves, M. F., and S. M. Watts-Taffe. 2002. "The Place of Word Consciousness in a Research-Based Vocabulary Program." In *What Research Has to Say About Reading Instruction*, edited by A. E. Farstrup and S. J. Samuels, 140–165. Newark, DE: International Reading Association.

Green, J. 2002. *Insect Societies*. London: Lorenz.

Greenberg, M. J. 2015. "Time to Reclassification: How Long Does It Take English Learner Students in Washington Road Map Districts to Develop English Proficiency?" REL 2015-092. Washington, DC: U.S. Department of Education, Institute of Education Sciences, National Center for Education Evaluation and Regional Assistance, Regional Educational Laboratory Northwest. Retrieved from http://ies.ed.gov/ncee/edlabs.

Greenleaf, C., R. Schoenbach, C. Cziko, and F. Mueller. 2001. "Apprenticing Adolescent Readers to Academic Literacy." *Harvard Educational Review* 71: 79–129.

Grolnick, W. S., and R. M. Ryan. 1989. "Parent Styles Associated with Children's Self-Regulation and Competence in School." *Journal of Educational Psychology* 81: 143–154.

Grolnick, W. S, R. M. Ryan, and E. L. Deci. 1991. "The Inner Resources for School Achievement Motivational Mediators of Children's Perceptions of Their Parents." *Journal of Educational Psychology* 83: 508–517.

Gunning, T. G. 2014. *Assessing and Correcting Reading and Writing Difficulties: A Student-Centered Approach*, 5th ed. Boston: Pearson.

Guthrie, J. T., S. L. Klauda, and A. N. Ho. 2013. "Modeling the Relationships Among Reading Instruction, Motivation, Engagement, and Achievement for Adolescents." *Reading Research Quarterly* 48: 9–26.

Guthrie, J. T., S. L. Klauda, and D. Morrison. 2012. "Motivation, Achievement, and Classroom Contexts for Information Book Reading." In *Adolescents' Engagement in Academic Literacy*, edited by J. T Guthrie, A. Wigfield, and S. L. Klauda, 1–52. College Park: University of Maryland.

Guthrie, J. T., A. McRae, and S. L. Klauda. 2007. "Contributions of Concept-Oriented Reading Instruction to Knowledge About Interventions for Motivations in Reading." *Educational Psychologist* 42 (4): 237–250. doi:10.1080/00461520701621087.

Guthrie, J. T., K. McGough, L. Bennett, and M. E. Rice. 1996. "Concept-Oriented Reading Instruction: An Integrated Curriculum to Develop Motivations and Strategies for Reading." In *Developing Engaged Readers in School and Home Communities,* edited by L. Baker, P. Afflerbach, and D. Reinking, 165–190. Hillsdale, NJ: Erlbaum.

Guthrie, J. T., and J. McPeake. 2013. "Literacy Engagement: The Missing Link." In *Quality Reading Instruction in the Age of Common Core Standards,* edited by S. Neuman and L. Gambrell, 162–175. Newark, DE: International Reading Association.

Guthrie, J. T., P. Van Meter, A. McCann, A. Wigfield, L. Bennett, C. Poundstone, and A. Mitchell. 1996. "Growth of Literacy Engagement: Changes in Motivation and Strategies During Concept-Oriented Reading Strategy." *Reading Research Quarterly* 31: 306–325.

Guthrie, J. T., and A. Wigfield. 1999. "How Motivation Fits into a Science of Reading." *Scientific Studies of Reading* 3: 199–205.

———. 2000. "Engagement and Motivation in Reading." In *Handbook of Reading Research,* vol. 3, edited by M. Kamil, P. Barr, P. Mosenthal, and P. Pearson, 403–422. New York: Longman.

Guthrie, J. T., A. Wigfield, P. Barbosa, K. C. Perencevich, A. Taboada, M. H. Davis, S. Tonks. 2004. "Increasing Reading Comprehension and Engagement Through Concept-Oriented Reading Instruction." *Journal of Educational Psychology* 96 (3): 403–423. doi:10.1037/0022-0663.96.3.403.

Guthrie, J. T., A. Wigfield, and S. L. Klauda. 2012. *Adolescents' Engagement in Academic Literacy.* Retrieved from www.cori.umd.edu/research-publications/2012_adolescents _engagement_ebook.pdf.

Guthrie, J. T., A. Wigfield, and K. C. Perencevich. 2004. *Motivating Reading Comprehension Concept-Oriented Reading Instruction.* Mahwah, NJ: Erlbaum.

Guthrie, J. T., A. Wigfield, and W. You. 2012. "Instructional Contexts for Engagement and Achievement in Reading." In *Handbook of Research on Student Engagement,* edited by S. Christensen, A. Reschly, and C. Wylie, 601–635. New York: Springer Science.

Hall, K. M., and B. L. Sabey. 2007. "Focus on the Facts: Using Informational Texts Effectively in Early Elementary Classrooms." *Early Childhood Education Journal* 35: 261–268. http://dx.doi.org/10.1007/s10643-007-0187-2.

Halvorsen, A. L., N. K. Duke, K. A. Brugar, M. K. Block, S. L. Strachan, M. B. Berka, and J. M. Brown. 2012. "Narrowing the Achievement Gap in Second-Grade Social Studies and Content Area Literacy: The Promise of a Project-Based Approach." *Theory & Research in Social Education* 40 (3): 198–229. doi:10.1080/00933104.2012.705954.

Hannon, P., and J. McNally. 1986. "Children's Understanding and Cultural Factors in Reading Test Performance." *Educational Review* 38 (3): 237–246. doi:10.1080/0013191860380304.

Harper, C., and E. de Jong. 2004. "Misconceptions About Teaching English-Language Learners." *Journal of Adolescent & Adult Literacy* 48 (2): 152–162.

Harper, D. 2016. *Etymology Online.* Retrieved from www.etymonline.com.

Harvey, S., and A. Goudvis. 2007. *Strategies That Work: Teaching Comprehension for Understanding and Engagement,* 2nd ed. Portland, ME: Stenhouse.

Heller, R., and C. Greenleaf. 2007. *Literacy Instruction in the Content Areas: Getting to the Core of Middle and High School Improvement.* Washington, DC: Alliance for Excellent Education.

Herber, H. L. 1970. *Teaching Reading in Content Areas.* Englewood Cliffs, NJ: Prentice-Hall.

Hoffman, D. E. 1973. "Students' Expectations and Performance in a Simulation Game." Unpublished PhD diss., Stanford University.

Hu, M., and I. S. P. Nation. 2000. "Unknown Vocabulary Density and Reading Comprehension." *Reading in a Foreign Language* 13: 403–430.

Hutchinson, J. M., H. E. Whiteley, C. D. Smith, and L. Connors. 2003. "The Developmental Progression of Comprehension-Related Skills in Children Learning EAL." *Journal of Research in Reading* 26: 19–32.

Isakson, R., and J. Miller. 1976. "Sensitivity to Syntactic and Semantic Cues in Good and Poor Comprehenders." *Journal of Educational Psychology* 68: 787–792.

Ivey, G., and P. H. Johnston. 2013. "Engagement with Young Adult Literature: Outcomes and Processes. *Reading Research Quarterly* 48 (3): 255–275. http://doi.org/10.1002/rrq.46.

Jacobs, J., S. Lanza, D. W. Osgood, J. S. Eccles, and A. Wigfield. 2002. "Changes in Children's Self-Competence and Values: Gender and Domain Differences Across Grades One Through Twelve." *Child Development* 73 (2): 509–527. doi:10.1111/1467-8624.00421.

Jeong, J., J. S. Gaffney, and J. O. Choi. 2010. "Availability and Use of Informational Text in Second-, Third-, and Fourth-Grade Classrooms." *Research in the Teaching of Children* 44 (4): 435–456.

Jimenez, R. 1997. "The Strategic Reading Abilities and Potential of Five Low-Literacy Latina/o Readers in Middle School." *Reading Research Quarterly* 32 (3): 224–243. doi:10.1598/RRQ.32.3.1.

Jimenez, R., G. Garcia, and D. Pearson. 1996. "The Reading Strategies of Bilingual Latina/o Students Who Are Successful English Readers: Opportunities and Obstacles." *Reading Research Quarterly* 31 (1): 90–112. doi:10.1598/RRQ.31.1.5.

Johnson, D., and R. Johnson. 1985. "Classroom Conflict: Controversy Versus Debate in Learning Groups." *American Educational Research Journal* 22 (2): 237–256.

Johnson-Laird, P. 1983. *Mental Models: Towards a Cognitive Science of Language, Inference, and Consciousness.* Cambridge, MA: Harvard University Press.

Kamil, M. 2003. *Adolescents and Literacy: Reading for the 21st Century.* Washington, DC: Alliance for Excellent Education.

Keene, E. O., and S. Zimmermann. 2007. *Mosaic of Thought: The Power of Comprehension Strategy Instruction,* 2nd ed. Portsmouth, NH: Heinemann.

Kennedy, J. 1996. *Word Stems: A Dictionary.* New York: Soho.

Kieffer, M., and N. K. Lesaux. 2012. "Development of Morphological Awareness and Vocabulary Knowledge in Spanish-Speaking Language Minority Learners: A Parallel Process Latent Growth Curve Model." *Applied Psycholinguistics* 33 (01): 23–54. doi:10.1017/S0142716411000099.

Kintsch, W. 2004. "The Construction-Integration Model of Text Comprehension and Its Implications for Instruction." In *Theoretical Models and Processes of Reading,* 5th ed., edited by R. Ruddell and N. Unrau. Newark, DE: International Reading Association.

Klingner, J., and S. Vaughn. 1999. "Promoting Reading Comprehension, Content Learning, and English Acquisition Through Collaborative Strategic Reading (CSR)." *The Reading Teacher* 52: 738–747.

Klingner, J., S. Vaughn, M. Arguelles, M. Tejero Hughes, and S. Ahwee Leftwich. 2004. "Collaborative Strategic Reading: 'Real-World' Lessons from Classroom Teachers." *Remedial and Special Education* 25 (53): 291–302.

Klingner, J., S. Vaughn, and J. S. Schumm. 1998. "Collaborative Strategic Reading During Social Studies in Heterogeneous Fourth-Grade Classrooms." *Elementary School Journal* 99: 3–22.

Kops, D. 2011. *Native Americans of the Plains.* Pelham, NY: Benchmark Education.

Krashen, S. 1985. *The Input Hypothesis: Issues and Implications.* New York: Longman.

———. 1989. "We Acquire Vocabulary and Spelling by Reading: Additional Evidence for the Input Hypothesis." *The Modern Language Journal* 73 (4): 440–464.doi:10 .1111/j.1540-4781.1989.tb05325.x.

———. 2004. *The Power of Reading: Insights from the Research*, 2nd ed. Westport, CT: Libraries Unlimited.

Kucan, L., and I. Beck. 1997. "Thinking Aloud and Reading Comprehension Research." *Review of Educational Research* 67 (3): 271–299.

Lanauze, M., and C. Snow. 1989. "The Relation Between First- and Second-Language Writing Skills: Evidence from Puerto Rican Elementary School Children in Bilingual Programs." *Linguistics and Education* 1: 323–339.

Landau, E. 2006. *The Homestead Act.* Danbury, CT: Children's Press.

Lesaux, N. 2012. "Reading and Reading Instruction for Children from Low-Income and Non-English-Speaking Households." *Future of Children* 22 (2): 73–88.

———. 2013. *Should Families of English Language Learners Have an English-only Rule at Home?* Retrieved from http://www.reading.org/general/Publications /blog/LRP/literacyresearchpanel/2013/06/10/should-families-of-English-language -learners-have-an-English-only-rule-at-home.

Lesaux, N., and E. Geva. 2006. "Synthesis: Development of Literacy in Language Minority Learners." In *Developing Literacy in a Second Language: Report of the National Literacy Panel,* edited by D. August and T. Shanahan, 53–74. Mahwah, NJ: Erlbaum.

Lesaux, N., M. Kieffer, S. Faller, and J. Kelley. 2010. "The Effectiveness and Ease of Implementation of an Academic Vocabulary Intervention for Linguistically Diverse Students in Urban Middle Schools." *Reading Research Quarterly* 45 (2): 196–228. doi:10.2307/20697183.

Long, M. 1996. "The Role of the Linguistic Environment in Second Language Acquisition." In *Handbook of Second Language Acquisition,* edited by W. Ritchie and T. Bhatia, 413–468. San Diego: Academic Press.

Maile, R. 2004. *The Pueblos: People of the Southwest.* Washington, DC: National Geographic Society.

———. 2007. *The Iroquois: People of the Northeast.* Monterrey, CA: National Geographic School Publishing.

Mancilla-Martinez, J., and N. Lesaux. 2010. "Predictors of Reading Comprehension for Struggling Readers: The Case of Spanish-Speaking Language Minority Learners." *Journal of Educational Psychology* 102 (3): 701–711. doi:10.1037/a0019135.

———. 2011a. "Early Home Language Use and Later Vocabulary Development." *Journal of Educational Psychology* 103 (3): 535–546. doi:10.1037/a0023655.

———. 2011b. "The Gap Between Spanish Speakers' Word Reading and Word Knowledge: A Longitudinal Study." *Child Development* 82 (5): 1544–1560. doi:10 .1111/j.1467-8624.2011.01633.x.

Manset-Williamson, G., M. Dunn, R. Hinshaw, and J. Nelson. 2008. "The Impact of Self-Questioning Strategy Use on the Text-Reader Assisted Comprehension of Students with Reading Disabilities." *International Journal of Special Education* 23 (1): 123–135.

Marzano, R., and D. Pickering. 2005. *Building Academic Vocabulary: Teacher's Manual.* Alexandria, VA: Association for Supervision and Curriculum Development.

McGowen, T. 1999. *African-Americans in the Old West.* Danbury, CT: Children's Press.

McKeown, R., and J. Gentilucci. 2007. "Think-Aloud Strategy: Metacognitive Development and Monitoring Comprehension in the Middle School Second-Language Classroom." *Journal of Adolescent and Adult Literacy* 51: 136–147.

Meece, J. 1991. "The Classroom Context and Children's Motivational Goals." In *Advances in Achievement Motivation Research,* vol. 7, edited by M. Maehr and P. Pintrich, 261–285. New York: Academic Press.

Meece, J., P. Blumenfeld, and R. Hoyle. 1988. "Students' Goal Orientations and Cognitive Engagement in Classroom Activities." *Journal of Educational Psychology* 80: 514–523.

Merriam-Webster. n.d. In *Merriam Webster Online.* Retrieved January 2016, http://www .wordcentral.com.

Molden, D., and C. Dweck. 2000. "Meaning and Motivation." In *Intrinsic Motivation,* ed. C. Sansone and J. Harackiewicz. San Diego: Academic Press.

Moll, L., and N. González. 1994. "Lessons from Research with Language-Minority Children." *Journal of Reading Behavior* 26 (4): 439–456.

Morgan, P., and D. Fuchs. 2007. "Is There a Bidirectional Relationship Between Children's Reading Skills and Reading Motivation?" *Exceptional Children* 73 (2): 165–183.

Moss, B. 2005. "Making a Case and a Place for Effective Content Area Literacy Instruction in the Elementary Grades." *The Reading Teacher* 59 (1): 46–55. http://doi.org/10.1598 /RT.59.1.5.

Nagy, W., P. Herman, and R. Anderson. 1985. "Learning Words from Context." *Reading Research Quarterly* 20 (2): 233–253. doi:10.2307/747758.

Nagy, W., and J. Scott. 2000. "Vocabulary Processes." In *Handbook of Reading Research,* vol. 3, edited by R. Barr, M. Kamil, P. Mosenthal, and P. Pearson, 269–284. Mahwah, NJ: Erlbaum.

Nagy, W., and D. Townsend. 2012. "Words as Tools: Learning Academic Vocabulary as Language Acquisition." *Reading Research Quarterly* 47 (1): 91–108. doi:10.1002 /RRQ.011.

Nakamoto, J., K. Lindsey, and F. Manis. 2007. "A Longitudinal Analysis of English Language Learners' Word Decoding and Reading Comprehension." *Reading and Writing* 20 (7): 691–719. doi:10.1007/s11145-006-9045-7.

National Academies Press. 2004. "Engaging Schools: Fostering High School Students' Motivation to Learn."

National Assessment Governing Board. 2010. *Reading Framework for the 2011 National Assessment of Educational Progress* (No. ED-02-R-0007).

National Center for Education Statistics (NCES). 2011. *Status and Trends in the Education of Racial and Ethnic Minorities.* Retrieved from http://nces.ed.gov/pubs2010/2010015/tables/table_8_2a.asp.

———. 2014. *The Condition of Education.* Retrieved from http://nces.ed.gov/pubs2014/2014083.pdf.

National Governors Association Center for Best Practices, and Council of Chief State School Officers. 2010. *Common Core State Standards.* Washington, DC: National Governors Association Center for Best Practices, Council of Chief State School Officers.

National Reading Panel. 2000. *Teaching Children to Read: An Evidence-Based Assessment of the Scientific Research Literature on Reading and Its Implications for Reading Instruction.* NIH Pub. No. 00-4769. Jessup, MD: National Institute for Literacy.

Ness, M. 2009. "Reading Comprehension Strategies in Secondary Content-Area Classrooms: Teacher Use of and Attitudes Toward Reading Comprehension Instruction." *Reading Horizons* 49 (2): 143–166.

———. 2013. "Unpark Those Questions: Use Students' Own Curiosity to Get Them to Investigate Informational Text." *Educational Leadership* 71 (3): 74–76.

Noddings, N. 1989. "Theoretical and Practical Concerns About Small Groups in Mathematics." *Elementary School Journal* 89: 607–623.

Nuland, L., A. Taboada Barber, T. Murray, and S. Groundwater. 2014. "Exploring Colonial America: Teaching History Through Literacy for Grade 6 Using the GAUGE Strategy." *IRA Bridges: Instructional Units for the Engaging Classroom,* 1–15. http://doi.org/10.1598/bridges.7011.

O'Brien, D., R. Stewart, and E. Moje. 1995. "Why Content Literacy Is Difficult to Infuse into the Secondary School: Complexities of Curriculum, Pedagogy, and School Culture." *Reading Research Quarterly* 30 (3): 442–463.

Oller, D., and R. Eilers. 2002. *Language and Literacy in Bilingual Children.* Clevedon, UK: Multilingual Matters. Retrieved from http://site.ebrary.com/id/10022456.

Pajares, F., and T. Urdan. 2006. *Self-Efficacy Beliefs of Adolescents.* Greenwich, CT: Information Age Publishing.

Palincsar, A., and A. Brown. 1984. "Reciprocal Teaching of Comprehension-Fostering and Comprehension-Monitoring Activities." *Cognition and Instruction* 1: 117–175.

Pappas, C. 2006. "The Information Book Genre: Its Role in Integrated Science Literacy Research and Practice." *Reading Research Quarterly* 41 (2): 226–250. doi:10.1598/RRQ.41.2.

Passel, J., and D. Cohn. 2008. *Population Projections: 2005–2050.* Washington, DC: Pew Hispanic Center. Retrieved from http://pewhispanic.org/files/reports/85.pdf.

Pearson, P. 2013. "Research Foundations of the Common Core State Standards in English Language Arts." In *Quality Reading Instruction in the Age of Common Core Standards,* edited by S. Neuman and L. Gambrell, 237–262. Newark, DE: International Reading Association.

Pearson, P., and M. Gallagher. 1983. "The Instruction of Reading Comprehension." *Contemporary Educational Psychology* 8: 317–344.

Pearson, P., E. Moje, and C. Greenleaf. 2010. "Literacy and Science: Each in the Service of the Other." *Science* 328 (5977): 459–463. doi:10.1126/science.1182595.

Perry, R., J. Chipperfield, S. Hladkyj, R. Pekrun, and J. Hamm. 2014. "Attribution-Based Treatment Interventions in Some Achievement Settings." In *Advances in Motivation and Achievement*, vol. 18, edited by S. Karabenick and T. Urdan. Bingley, UK: Emerald Publishing.

Pica, T. 1994. "Research on Negotiation: What Does It Reveal About Second-Language Learning Conditions, Processes, and Outcomes?" *Language Learning* 44: 493–527. doi:10.1111/j.1467–1770.1994.tb01115.x.

Pintrich, P. 2000. "An Achievement Goal Theory Perspective on Issues in Motivation Terminology, Theory, and Research." *Contemporary Educational Psychology* 25 (1): 92–104. doi:10.1006/ceps.1999.1017.

Pressley, M. 2000. "What Should Comprehension Instruction Be the Instruction Of?" In *Handbook of Reading Research,* vol. 3, edited by M. Kamil, P. Mosenthal, P. Pearson, and R. Barr, 545–561. Mahwah, NJ: Erlbaum.

Pressley, M., and P. Afflerbach. 1995. *Verbal Protocols of Reading: The Nature of Constructively Responsive Reading.* Hillsdale, NJ: Erlbaum.

Pressley, M., P. El-Dinary, I. Gaskins, T. Schuder, J. Bergman, J. Almasi, and R. Brown. 1992. "Beyond Direct Explanation: Transactional Instruction of Reading Comprehension Strategies." *Elementary School Journal* 92 (5): 513–555.

Pressley, M., and K. Harris. 2006. "Cognitive Strategies Instruction: From Basic Research to Classroom Instruction." In *Handbook of Educational Psychology*, 2nd ed., edited by P. Alexander and P. Winne, 265–286. Mahwah, NJ: Erlbaum.

Proctor, C., M. Carlo, D. August, and C. Snow. 2005. "Native Spanish-Speaking Children Reading in English: Toward a Model of Comprehension." *Journal of Educational Psychology* 97 (2): 246–256. doi:10.1037/0022-0663.97.2.246.

Proctor, C., B. Dalton, and D. Grisham. 2007. "Scaffolding English Language Learners and Struggling Readers in a Universal Literacy Environment with Embedded Strategy Instruction and Vocabulary Support." *Journal of Literacy Research* 39 (1): 71–93.

Purcell-Gates, V., N. K. Duke, and J. Martineau. 2007. "Learning to Read and Write Genre-Specific Text: Roles of Authentic Experience and Explicit Teaching." *Reading Research Quarterly* 42 (1): 8–45.

Ramsden, N. 2012. *Word Searcher*. Retrieved from www.neilramsden.co.uk/spelling/searcher/index.html.

Reeve, J., and H. Jang. 2006. "What Teachers Say and Do to Support Students' Autonomy During a Learning Activity." *Journal of Educational Psychology* 98 (1): 209–218. http://doi.org/10.1037/0022-0663.98.1.209.

Riches, C., and F. Genesee. 2006. "Literacy: Crosslinguistic and Crossmodal Issues." In *Educating English Language Learners: A Synthesis of Research Evidence,* edited by F. Genesee, K. Lindholm-Leary, W. Saunders, and D. Christian. Cambridge, UK: Cambridge University Press.

Richey, L., A. Taboada Barber, T. Whiting, and S. Groundwater. 2014. *Exploring Colonial America: Teaching History Through Literacy for Grade 6 Using the GAUGE Strategy.* Paper presented at the 59th International Reading Association (IRA), New Orleans, LA, April.

Rosenholtz, S. 1985. "Treating Problems of Academic Status." In *Status, Rewards, and Influence,* edited by J. Berger and M. Zelditch Jr., 445–470. San Francisco: Jossey-Bass.

Rosenshine, B. 1980. "How Time Is Spent in Elementary Classrooms." In *Time to Learn,* edited by C. Denham and A. Lieberman, 107–126. Washington, DC: National Institute of Education.

Rosenshine, B., C. Meister, and S. Chapman. 1996. "Teaching Students to Generate Questions: A Review of the Intervention Studies." *Review of Educational Research* 66 (2): 181–221.

Rossi, A. 2002. *Two Cultures Meet: Native American and European.* Washington, DC: National Geographic Society.

Rumelhart, D. 1984. "Schemata and the Cognitive System." In *Handbook of Social Cognition,* vol. 1, edited by R. Wyer and T. Srull, 161–188. Mahwah, NJ: Erlbaum.

———. 1994. "Toward an Interactive Model of Reading." In *Theoretical Models and Processes of Reading,* 4th ed., edited by R. Ruddell, M. Ruddell, and H. Singer, 864–894. Newark, DE: International Reading Association.

Ryan, R. 1993. "Agency and Organization: Intrinsic Motivation, Autonomy, and the Self in Psychological Development." In *Nebraska Symposium on Motivation,* vol. 40, *Developmental Perspectives on Motivation,* edited by J. Jacobs, 1–56. Lincoln: University of Nebraska Press.

Saddler, B., and S. Graham. 2007. "The Relationship Between Writing Knowledge and Writing Performance Among More and Less Skilled Writers." *Reading & Writing Quarterly* 23 (3): 231–247. doi:10.1080/10573560701277575.

Saenz, L., and L. Fuchs. 2002. "Examining the Reading Difficulty of Secondary Students with Learning Disabilities: Expository Versus Narrative Text." *Remedial and Special Education* 23 (1): 31–41.

Santella, A. 2001a. *The Inuit.* New York: Children's Press.

———. 2001b. *The Lakota Sioux.* New York: Children's Press.

Scanlon, D., D. Deshler, and J. Schumaker. 1996. "Can a Strategy Be Taught and Learned in Secondary Inclusive Classrooms?" *Learning Disabilities Research and Practice* 11: 41–57.

Scardamalia, M., and C. Bereiter. 1992. "Text-Based and Knowledge Based Questioning by Children." *Cognition and Instruction* 9 (3): 177–199.

Schmar-Dobler, E. 2003. "Reading on the Internet: The Link Between Literacy and Technology." *Journal of Adolescent & Adult Literacy* 47 (1): 80–85.

Silverman, R., and S. Hines. 2009. "The Effects of Multimedia-Enhanced Instruction on the Vocabulary of English-Language Learners and Non-English-Language Learners in Pre-Kindergarten Through Second Grade." *Journal of Educational Psychology* 101 (2): 305–314. ERIC Document Reproduction Service No. EJ835042.

Sjostrom, C. L., and V. C. Hare. 1984. "Teaching High School Students to Identify Main Ideas in Expository Text." *The Journal of Educational Research* 78 (2): 114–118.

Skinner, E. A., and M. J. Belmont. 1993. "Motivation in the Classroom: Reciprocal Effects of Teacher Behavior and Student Engagement Across the School Year." *Journal of Educational Psychology* 85 (4): 571–581. doi:10.1037/0022-0663.85.4.571.

Slavin, R. E., C. Lake, B. Chambers, A. Cheung, and S. Davis. 2009. "Effective Reading Programs for the Elementary Grades: A Best-Evidence Synthesis." *Review of Educational Research* 79: 1391–1466. doi:10.3102/0034654309341374.

Snow, C. 2013. "Cold Versus Warm Close Reading: Stamina and the Accumulation of Misdirection." *Literacy Daily* (blog), International Literacy Association, June 6. www.literacyworldwide.org/blog/literacy-daily/2013/06/06/cold-versus-warm-close-reading-stamina-and-the-accumulation-of-misdirection.

Snow, C. E., M. V. Porsche, P. O. Tabors, and S. R. Harris. 2007. *Is Literacy Enough? Pathways to Academic Success for Adolescents.* Baltimore: Brookes.

Stahl, S. A. 1999. *Vocabulary Development.* Cambridge, MA: Brookline Books.

Stahl, S. A., and M. M. Fairbanks. 1986. "The Effects of Vocabulary Instruction: A Model-Based Meta-Analysis." *Review of Educational Research* 56 (1): 72–110. doi:10.3102/00346543056001072.

Stahl, S. A., and W. E. Nagy. 2006. *Teaching Word Meanings.* Mahwah, NJ: Erlbaum.

Stanovich, K. E. 1986. "Matthew Effects in Reading: Some Consequences of Individual Differences in the Acquisition of Literacy." *Reading Research Quarterly* 21 (4): 360–407. doi:10.1598/RRQ.21.4.1.

Stefanou, C. R., K. C. Perencevich, M. DiCintio, and J. C. Turner. 2004. "Supporting Autonomy in the Classroom: Ways Teachers Encourage Student Decision Making and Ownership." *Educational Psychologist* 39 (2): 97–110. doi:10.1207/s15326985ep3902_2.

Sternberg, R. J. 1987. "Most Vocabulary Is Learned from Context." In *The Nature of Vocabulary Acquisition*, edited by M. G. McKeown and M. E. Curtis, 89–105. Hillsdale, NJ: Erlbaum.

Stipek, D., and J. H. Gralinski. 1996. "Children's Beliefs About Intelligence and School Performance." *Journal of Educational Psychology* 88 (3): 397–407. doi:10.1037/0022-0663.88.3.397.

Stoddart, T., A. Pinal, M. Latzke, and D. Canaday. 2002. "Integrating Inquiry Science and Language Development for English Language Learners." *Journal of Research in Science Teaching* 39 (8): 664–687.

Sweet, A. P., J. T. Guthrie, and M. M. Ng. 1998. "Teacher Perceptions and Student Reading Motivation." *Journal of Educational Psychology* 90 (2): 210–223. doi:10.1037/0022-0663.90.2.210.

Taboada, A. 2009. "English Language Learners, Vocabulary, and Reading Comprehension: What We Know and What We Need to Know." *Yearbook of the College Reading Association* 30: 307–322.

Taboada, A., S. Bianco, and V. Bowerman. 2012. "Text-Based Questioning: A Comprehension Strategy to Build English Language Learners' Content Knowledge." *Literacy Research & Instruction* 51 (2): 87–109.

Taboada, A., M. M. Buehl, J. Kidd, and E. Sturtevant. 2010. "Fostering Reading Engagement in English-Monolingual Students and English Language Learners Through a History Curriculum." Awarded FY 2010, Reading and Writing Education Research grants competition, Institute of Education Sciences (IES).

Taboada, A., M. M. Buehl, J. K. Kidd, E. Sturtevant, L. Richey, and J. Beck. 2011. "Reading Engagement in Social Studies: The Evolution a Middle School Content-Area Literacy Curriculum." Paper presented at the Literacy Research Association (LRA), Jacksonville, FL.

Taboada, A., and J. T. Guthrie. 2004. "Contributions of Student Questioning and Prior Knowledge to Construction of Knowledge from Reading Information Text." *Journal of Literacy Research* 38 (1): 1–35.

Taboada, A., J. Kidd, and S. Tonks. 2009. "A Qualitative Look at English Language Learners' Perceptions of Autonomy Support in a Literacy Classroom." Paper presented at the annual meeting of the National Reading Conference (NRC), Albuquerque, NM.

———. 2010. "English Language Learners' Perceptions of Autonomy Support in a Literacy Classroom." *Research in the Schools* 17 (2): 39–53. Retrieved from http://mutex.gmu.edu/login?url=http://search.ebscohost.com/login.aspx?direct=true&db=ehh&AN=64433163&site=ehost-live&scope=site.

Taboada, A., D. Townsend, and M. J. Boynton. 2013. "Mediating Effects of Reading Engagement on the Reading Comprehension of Early Adolescent English Language Learners." *Reading & Writing Quarterly: Overcoming Learning Difficulties* 29 (4): 309–332. doi:10.1080/10573569.2013.741959.

Taboada, A., and V. Rutherford. 2011. "Developing Reading Comprehension and Academic Vocabulary for English Language Learners through Science Content: A Formative Experiment." *Reading Psychology* 32 (2): 113–157.

Taboada Barber, A., M. M. Buehl, J. K. Kidd, E. Sturtevant., L. N. Richey, and J. Beck. 2015. "Engagement in Social Studies: Exploring the Role of a Social Studies Literacy Intervention on Reading Comprehension, Reading Self-Efficacy, and Engagement in Middle School Students with Different Language Backgrounds." *Reading Psychology* 36 (1): 31–85. doi:10.1080/02702711.2013.815140.

Taboada Barber, A., and M. Gallagher. 2015. "Young Adolescents' Self-Regulated Reading in American History: Helping English Learners Become Engaged Readers." In *Self-Regulated Learning Interventions with At-Risk Youth: Enhancing Adaptability, Performance, and Well Being,* edited by T. J. Cleary. Washington, DC: American Psychological Association.

Taboada Barber, A., and E. M. Ramirez. (Under review.) "Growth of ELs' Reading Comprehension Strategies after Intensive Intervention."

Taboada Barber, A., L. N. Richey, and M. M. Buehl. 2013. "Promoting Comprehension and Motivation to Read in the Middle School Social Studies Classroom: Examples from a Research-Based Curriculum." In *Comprehension Strategies to Promote Adolescent Literacy in the Content-Areas for the Inclusive Classroom,* edited by R. T. Boon and V. Spencer. Baltimore: Brookes.

Taylor, B. 2000. *Elephants.* London: Southwater/Anness.

Taylor, B. M. 1980. "Children's Memory for Expository Text after Reading." *Reading Research Quarterly* 15: 399–411.

Taylor, B. M., P. D. Pearson, K. Clark, and S. Walpole. 2000. "Effective Schools and Accomplished Teachers: Lessons about Primary-Grade Reading Instruction in Low-Income Schools." *Elementary School Journal* 101: 121–165.

Templeton, S. 2012. "The Vocabulary–Spelling Connection and Generative Instruction: Morphological Knowledge at the Intermediate Grades and Beyond." In *Vocabulary Instruction: Research to Practice,* 2nd ed., edited by E. J. Kame'enui and J. F. Baumann, 116–138. New York: Guilford.

Templeton, S., D. Bear, M. Invernizzi, and F. Johnston. 2010. *Vocabulary Their Way: Word Study with Middle and Secondary Students.* Boston: Pearson.

Therrien, W. J., K. Wickstrom, and K. Jones. 2006. "Effect of a Combined Repeated Reading and Question Generation Intervention on Reading Achievement." *Learning Disabilities Research and Practice* 21 (2): 89–97.

Thorndike, E. L. 1917. "Reading as Reasoning: A Study of Mistakes in Paragraph Reading." *Journal of Educational Psychology* 8 (6): 323.

Torgesen, J. K., D. D. Houston, L. M. Rissman, S. M. Decker, G. Roberts, S. Vaughn, and M. O. Rivera. 2007. *Academic Literacy Instruction for Adolescents: A Guidance Document from the Center on Instruction.* Portsmouth, NH: RMC Research Corporation, Center on Instruction.

Tudge, J. 1990. "Vygotsky: The Zone of Proximal Development and Peer Collaboration: Implications for Classroom Practice." In *Vygotsky and Education: Instructional Implications and Applications of Sociohistorical Psychology,* edited by L. Moll. New York: Columbia University Press.

U.S. Department of Education, Institute of Education Sciences, National Center for Education Statistics, National Assessment of Educational Progress (NAEP). 2011. *1992, 1994, 1998, 2000, 2002, 2003, 2005, 2007, 2009, and 2011 Reading Assessments.* Washington, DC: U.S. Department of Education.

U.S. Department of Education, Institute of Education Sciences, National Center for Education Statistics, National Assessment of Educational Progress (NAEP). 2013. *Reading Assessment Report Card* [Data tables]. Washington, DC: U.S. Department of Education. Retrieved from www.nationsreportcard.gov/reading_math_2013/files /Results_Appendix_Reading.pdf.

U.S. Department of Education, Institute of Education Sciences, National Center for Education Statistics (NCES). 2014. *The Condition of Education. English Language Learners.* Washington, DC: U.S. Department of Education. Retrieved from http://nces .ed.gov/programs/coe/indicator_cgf.asp.

Umbel, V. M., B. Z. Pearson, M. C. Fernandez, and D. K. Oller. 1992. "Measuring Bilingual Children's Receptive Vocabularies." *Child Development* 63 (4): 1012–1020. doi:10.1111/j.1467-8624.1992.tb01678.x.

Vaca, J., D. Lapp, and D. Fisher. 2011. "Designing and Assessing Productive Group Work in Secondary Schools." *Journal of Adolescent & Adult Literacy* 54 (5): 372–375. doi:10.1598/JAAL.54.5.7.

van den Broek, B. P., J. S. Lynch, J. Naslund, C. E. Ievers-Landis, and K. Verduin. 2003. "The Development of Comprehension of Main Ideas in Narratives: Evidence from the Selection of Titles." *Journal of Educational Psychology* 95: 707–718.

Vaughn, S., L. R. Martinez, S. Linan-Thompson, C. K. Reutebuch, C. D. Carlson, and D. J. Francis. 2009. "Enhancing Social Studies Vocabulary and Comprehension for Seventh-Grade English Language Learners: Findings from Two Experimental Studies." *Journal of Research on Educational Effectiveness* 2 (4): 297–324. doi:10.1080/19345740903167018.

WIDA Consortium. 2012. *WIDA Performance Definitions-Listening and Reading Grades K–12*. Retrieved from https://www.wida.us/standards/.

Wigfield, A., J. S. Eccles, U. Schiefele, R. W. Roeser, and P. Davis-Kean. 2006. "Development of Achievement Motivation." In *Social, Emotional, and Personality Development,* 6th ed., vol. 3, edited by N. Eisenberg, 933–1002. New York: Wiley.

Wigfield, A., and J. T. Guthrie. 1997. "Relation of Children's Motivation for Reading to the Amount and Breadth of Their Reading." *Journal of Educational Psychology* 89 (3): 420–432.

Wigfield, A., A. Mason-Singh, A. N. Ho, and J. T. Guthrie. 2014. "Intervening to Improve Children's Reading Motivation and Comprehension: Concept-Oriented Reading Instruction." In *Motivational Interventions: Advances in Motivation and Achievement,* edited by S. Karabenick and T. C. Urdan, 37–70. Bingley, UK: Emerald Group.

Wilkinson, I., and E. H. Son. 2011. "A Dialogic Turn in Research on Learning and Teaching to Comprehend." In *Handbook of Reading Research,* vol. 4, edited by M. L. Kamil, P. D. Pearson, E. B. Moje, and P. P. Afflerbach, 359–387. New York: Routledge.

Index